FROM
SaiNT
HiLDeGaRD'S
KITCHEN

FROM

SaiNT HiLDeGarD'S

* KITCHEN *

Foods OF Health
Foods OF Joy

JANY FOURNIER-ROSSET

TRANSLATED BY VICTORIA HÉBERT AND DENIS SABOURIN

Liguori
LIGUORI, MISSOURI

Published by Liguori Publications
Liguori, Missouri 63057-9999
To order, call 800-325-9521
www.liguori.org

Important Notice: This book is intended as an informational reference, not as a medical guide. Any plant, whether used as food or medicine, can cause an allergic reaction in some people. Do not take any unknown substances during pregnancy without consulting a physician. This guide is not intended as a substitute for medical treatment. The author and the publisher expressly disclaim any responsibility or liability in connection with the use of this book.

Library of Congress Cataloging-in-Publication Data

Fournier-Rosset, Jany.
    [Recettes de la joie avec Sainte Hildegard. English]
    From Saint Hildegard's kitchen : foods of health, foods of joy / Jany Fournier-Rosset ; translated by Victoria Hébert and Denis Sabourin. — 1st U.S. ed.
      p. cm.
    Includes index.
    ISBN 978-0-7648-1951-3
    1. Nutrition. 2. Natural foods. 3. Health. 4. Hildegard, Saint, 1098–1179.
I. Title.
RA784.F65213   1999
641.5.'63—dc21   99–23315

Printed in the United States of America

First published in France as *Les recettes de la joie avec sainte Hildegarde* by Éditions Téqui, Paris, France.

16 15 14 13 / 6 5 4 3
Second U.S. Edition

CONTENTS

INTRODUCTION

How wonderful it is to discover the secret of joy in the enlightened revelations of a twelfth-century Benedictine Abbess! Nine hundred years ago, in the Middle Ages, Hildegard of Bingen was granted, by means of heavenly visions, precious knowledge about human nutrition: while the "foods of sadness" sap our health and vitality, the "foods of joy" revitalize us and help preserve good health in every sphere: physical, spiritual, and psychological.

How can a simple dietary regimen succeed in preventing illness and producing radiant health? It does so by eliminating the foods that result in the "black bile" of sadness, as Saint Hildegard calls it, and eating those that prevent its accumulation. On the other hand, foods of joy chase sadness away and bring happiness and balm to our hearts.

The author, Jany Fournier-Rosset, is a lay oblate of Saint Benedict, married, a mother, and well known for her talents as an accomplished chef. She offers us an original selection of healthy and flavorful recipes, based upon the writings and teachings of Saint Hildegard.

SAINT HILDEGARD: A SHORT BIOGRAPHY

Born in 1098 in Bockelheim, Germany, of noble parents, Hildegard was the youngest of ten children. As custom dictated, she was dedicated to God at the age of eight. Her training and education was entrusted to Mother Jutta Von Spannheim, superior of the cloistered religious of Disidodenberg. She taught Hildegard to read, write, and even instructed her in Latin, educating her as well about the Benedictine rule.

It is said that Hildegard learned little from humans. Her complete and encompassing knowledge was said to come to her through visions, given to her directly from heaven.

Hildegard pronounced her vows with the cloistered Benedictines at the age of eighteen and later became the mistress of novices. A biographer said about her: "Hildegard was the first of the great German mystics; she was a prophet, a poet, a physician, and a political moralist who reprimanded popes, crowned heads, bishops, and laypersons alike; she was totally honest and demonstrated an infallible sense of justice."

Identified as a mystical visionary from the age of three, Hildegard astonished everyone when she described the markings of a calf while it was still inside its mother's womb: it was born with the exact markings the young Hildegard had indicated! Her visions were prophetic and, above all, mysterious.

Hildegard's visions increased in frequency, and she was asked by her superiors to write down what she saw. At first, she was afraid of this task, and she demurred. Her already shaky health worsened, and she saw this decline as a sign from God, a punishment for her initial refusal. She agreed to record her visions, first as a means to uplift her fellow religious, but later (at the age of forty-three), she received a directive from God to "write and tell" about her visions. With the support of her confessor, Father Volmar, a monk who later became her secretary, she began writing the *Scivias*, a book of visions that took more than ten years to complete. As soon as she began to write, her health improved. From then on, her life followed a pattern: sickness followed by the task of committing her visions to writing, followed by a return to health.

The first pages of the *Scivias* were then submitted to the Bishop of Mayence (some twenty-five kilometers north of the convent and the episcopal seat). An investigatory commission was set up to examine the documents and the visions they recorded. The commission later declared Hildegard's prophecies to be authentic directives from God.

Saint Bernard, the Abbot of Clairvaux, begged Pope Eugene III not to keep such a great source of enlightenment a secret. He recognized the validity of Hildegard's writings only after he read them in public to the cardinals, bishops, and theologians gathered at a Council in Trèves.

The books, songs, and guidelines written by Hildegard increased. She touched on many topics: theology, ethics, herbalism, medicine, physiology, biographies, poetry, and even music. She was in great demand as a teacher and sought after as an advisor by both lay and spiritual leaders.

All of her advice and writings came to her as messages, given to her directly from God. It is amazing to realize the scope of her knowledge, especially in the medical arena, when current practices of the time were far behind her enlightened "cures." She was the first woman in Europe to write books, to preach in public, to compose and distribute music, and also the first woman to gather and publish information with respect to the human body. This is incredible when we consider she lived in a society and in an era of total male dominance.

A woman of generally poor health (by all reports, including her own), she was of small stature, yet she was powerful in her impact on the people of her time. Her astounding gifts and power were truly amazing, and still are to this day.

At this point in her life (at the end of the year 1140), Hildegard sought to break away from the constraints of the traditional monastery. Having been named abbess of her Benedictine community at the age of thirty-six, upon the death of Mother Jutta, she sought to establish a fully devotional convent. After much opposition, she finally left, in 1150, and moved the entire convent out from under the auspices of the abbey into some deserted buildings across the river at Rupertsberg. In time, a mixed monastery, comprised of both nuns and monks and built by their very own hands, was established. She counted three of her siblings among her flock.

Little is known directly about the later years of Hildegard's life. What is known is that she was a prolific writer, a devoted religious, and a true mystic.

At her jubilee in 1998, Pope John Paul II said of Hildegard:

"...blessed early in her childhood with celestial gifts, she acquired profound knowledge of the mysteries of theology, medicine, music, and other arts. She wrote numerous books and brought a special enlightenment upon the relationship between redemption and creation...."

Saint Hildegard's Spirituality As It Relates to Her Teachings About a Healthy Diet

Above all, in spite of the variety of subjects she touched, Hildegard was firm in one major point of view—God is first in everything. All of her writings were a reflection of this fact and this fact alone. God is the source of all life; He was and is without beginning. He made the world and placed humanity at its center as an "exquisite jewel."

Hildegard held that as a result of sin, human beings become weak and fragile, as well as mortal. Inner conflicts were a result of human beings severing ties with nature and God. Disease resulted from this dichotomy, allowing sadness to produce, according to Hildegard, "black bile."

St. Isidore of Seville (ca. 560-636 A.D.) drew the link (first devised by Hippocrates) between the four elements and the four humors: "All diseases arise from the four humors, namely, blood, yellow bile, black bile and phlegm..." As long as these mixtures were kept in harmony with the four elements—air, water, fire, and earth—humankind remained healthy. Hildegard espoused this theory and stated that God alone blessed humankind with good health and balance. The four elements determine the constitution of the humors and, therefore, the state of health or illness. Everything works in harmony. Hildegard further stated that Adam's fall from grace into sin caused the ultimate upheaval in human physiology. "If black bile is stronger than the others…the person will tend to become angry, and illness and melancholy will set in," she said in her book *Causes and Cures*.

In the Middle Ages, people viewed the healing arts as being "in God's hands." The means to gain salvation were frequently indistinguishable from those used by the medicine of the time to return a person to health. All nature (and natural products and substances) came from God. It was he who healed the sick: Hildegard was only his medical and spiritual instrument.

Hildegard taught that the healing strength of plants was a function of their greenness, or *viriditas*, which is a gift from God. All of God's gifts are green, and from them flow the power to give or restore good health. This greenness is, in itself, a powerful life-force from God.

But a caution must be issued here: this greenness created by God can only benefit human beings when used according to strict guidelines, reasonably and only when necessary, and with the cooperation of the person being treated. This said, Hildegard and her writings became an essential link between God and good health.

Saint Paul tells us: "Do you not know that your body is a temple of the Holy Spirit within you, which you have from God, and that you are not your own? For you were bought with a price; therefore glorify God in your body" (1 Cor 6:19). We must neglect nothing to welcome our Creator, and, advises Hildegard, "…rejoicing in his inhabited world and delighting in the human race," and we must purify our bodies by consuming pure, wholesome foods.

The greatest founders of religious orders emphasized the value of good food, fasting as a purification of the body, and the observance of specific dietary guidelines. These practices played an essential role in spiritual health and illumination.

In his rule, Saint Benedict dedicated three of his seventy-two chapters to nutritional concerns: Chapter 39, "The Measure of Food;" Chapter 40, "The Measure of Drink;" and Chapter 43, "At What Time the Brothers Must Take Their Meals." He further discussed nutritional needs by outlining special diets for children, the sick, and elderly monks. Among his numerous works, one can find one entitled, *The Book of the Divine Subtleties of Divine Creatures*, which is an additional basis for the present book of recipes by Hildegard.

Hildegard taught that the Blessed Virgin Mary was the "mother of medicine." Mary, having been given the ultimate gift of mercy (the best medicine imaginable) was, according to Hildegard, "an exceedingly sweet plant in the air and dew and all green freshness." Whoever was weighed down by vices and illness should seek God's mercy through confession and penitence. In this way, sins and all "foulness" would be eliminated, in the same way as is digested food and drink.

Penitence is the refreshing green power of healing. Hildegard's works cite it as the "light of the soul" and as a remedy in itself. It is truly an all-powerful force. Tears of repentance cause an influx of greenness—that refreshing and rejuvenating creative green life force whose radiance rises to the Divine Light—so that *viriditas* once again wells up in the human soul.

Hildegard viewed life as the continuation of God's creation, and she saw health as a constant regeneration through God, an ongoing process that embraced and enjoined all areas of nature and spirituality.

Hildegard was also a proponent of moderation and discretion in all things, as expressed in the rule of Saint Benedict. As well, she took a systematic approach to religious and spiritual life based upon hygiene and proper nutrition.

God created all of humankind and gave them the whole world so they could work with nature (which lives in, yet transcends, all human beings). Our human obedience to God and to nature leads to salvation and good health. We then become partners with God in the ways of creation, a collaboration that leads to salvation.

Hildegard sang in the spirit of Song of Solomon 5:1: "Eat, friends, drink, and be drunk with love." In her own words, "Eat in faith from the body of God, who is the true medicine, drink in hope from the wine which is the cup of salvation, and be inebriated with love for Our Lord."

TIPS ABOUT HILDEGARD'S SPIRITUAL DIET AND THE PREPARATION OF FOOD

Hildegard makes us appreciate the virtues as well as the dangers of our surroundings. She classified foods and spices by their "character:" hot or cold, dry or humid and moist. The vital force is the greenness of foods.

It is quite a challenge to adapt teachings that were written in the Middle Ages to modern times. However, the recipes contained in this book conform to Hildegard's writings, as found in her book *Physica*. The recipes have been thoroughly tested and are comprised solely of those foods, spices, and herbs which possess the virtues of greenness, lightness, and digestibility; in other words, the "foods of joy" that Hildegard prefers for their subtle values. On the other hand, one must avoid consuming those foods which may be detrimental to human beings, unless one is willing to risk "disorder." Hence, the reader will not find any of the following foods in this book (as they may cause "disorder"): prepared meats, pork, leeks, raw onions, strawberries, plums, ginger on its own, or an excessive use of honey.

In following Hildegard's teachings about the close link between human beings and the universe, we suggest eating seasonal fruits and vegetables: they have been put on earth by nature for that single purpose, to feed us at that particular time alone. They compensate for the disequilibrium generated in the body by seasonal climates. If we eat food out-of-season, we risk health problems and an upset in the delicate balance of life forces.

The reader will also note that most recipes are prepared at lower cooking temperatures, as Hildegard instructed, so as not to brutalize the foods. Aluminum, copper, and pewter cooking vessels must be avoided because of the toxic salts they release.

Of all the ingredients used in the recipes in this book, the most important one is love. It is the single most important ingredient in any preparation. It gives even the most ordinary of dishes an incredible flavor. To cook with love is to offer one's own heart. To express one's affection through the preparation of that special dish is like "the dew of Hermon descending upon the heights of Zion" (Ps 133:3). It is a soothing balm for the heart, fortifying the body and giving comfort to the soul.

> "The earth which sustains humanity
> must not be injured, it must not be destroyed."
> *St. Hildegard of Bingen*

Introduction

BaSiC INGReDieNTS

In this section, certain basic ingredients used in this book of recipes will be described. Some readers may read this list and fail to recognize or know where to purchase these ingredients, which are basic to the success of the Hildegard's way of preparing foods. In truth, it is not difficult to find these ingredients, and most are available in your local natural food store, and some online. (At the end of this book, we will provide a list of such online addresses.) In the pages that follow, an explanation of the foods, herbs, and spices that bring joy are provided.

"Everywhere in creation,
trees, plants, animals, and gems,
there are mysterious healing forces,
which no person can know,
unless they are revealed to him by God."

St. Hildegard of Bingen

Foods That Bring Joy

Among the cereal grains usually used in Saint Hildegard's recipes, we find spelt and oats:

SPELT
(Triticum spelta)

Hildegard says the following about spelt: "Spelt is an excellent cereal grain, of a warm nature, big and full of strength, and gentler than all of the other cereal grains: those who eat it find that they have better skin and blood. It gives one a happy outlook and a sense of exhilaration. It is good no matter what form of the grain we choose to use, whether as a bread or as an ingredient in any recipe."

The origins of spelt go back over nine thousand years. Currently, it is especially useful for those who are sensitive to wheat. It may be readily substituted for wheat in any recipe, and vice versa, and adds a subtle nutlike flavor. It is high in the ratio of complex versus simple carbohydrates and in vitamin B (useful to reduce stress and increase levels of energy). It is reported to help minimize muscle pain and facilitate quicker healing. High in protein (including the eight essential amino acids), it is an essential element in a diet to promote adequate cell maintenance.

OATS
(Avena sativa)
ALSO KNOWN AS COMMON OATS, GROATS

Although not suitable for those who are ill, oats are equally important as an excellent cereal grain that brings joy: "It constitutes a healthy food for those people in good health: it gives them a joyful soul; a clear head, good color, and healthy skin," says Saint Hildegard.

In the Middle Ages, oats were seen as a good source of nutrition. Medicinally, they were often given as a treatment for loss of appetite, exhaustion, sleeplessness, and loss of strength after an illness. Oat grains were sometimes roasted to make a drink that relieved constipation. Mattresses made of oats (along with straw) were thought to ease arthritic pains.

Saint Hildegard recommends oats as part of a steaming sauna bath for those whose thoughts need calming. One should pour the water in which oats have been prepared over hot rocks. This treatment will help the person whose mind is racing and who is preoccupied with crazy thoughts.

Oats were sometimes made into a poultice that helped to relieve lumbago, skin problems, and sciatica. Even today, a poultice made of oats and applied to the face is thought to stave off wrinkles.

As a cereal grain, oats are popular ingredients in pastries, porridge, gruel, and pancakes.

FENNEL

(Foeniculum vulgare)

ALSO KNOWN AS SWEET FENNEL, WILD FENNEL

When speaking about vegetables, Saint Hildegard gives a special place to fennel: "Fennel contains a gentle warmth, its nature being neither dry nor cold. Eaten raw, it is not harmful. And, no matter what way we choose to eat it, it makes our hearts joyful; it gives mankind a gentle warmth of nature, a good 'sweat;' and ensures good digestion. Its seeds are equally good for health if added to other plants in medications.

"Whoever eats fennel on a daily basis, first thing in the morning on an empty stomach, will find that it reduces phlegm and freshens the breath as well as ensuring good eyesight, thanks to its warm nature and good basic properties."

Basic Ingredients

Other curative uses for fennel were to improve the flow of milk in nursing mothers and added to foods as an antidote to fatness. Others recommended fennel as a remedy for poisonous mushrooms.

From a culinary standpoint, fennel was added to salads and herbal teas. It was also used in sauces, stews, soups, and stuffings. It adds a licorice flavor to breads and pastries.

In medieval monasteries, fennel seeds were taken to reduce hunger pangs on fast days; and it was hung over doors or fastened to keyholes to freshen the air.

NETTLE
(Urtica dioica)
ALSO KNOWN AS COMMON NETTLE OR STINGING NETTLE

The name "nettle" comes from the Old English words for needle, as a result of the plant's sting. Saint Hildegard characterized nettle as a "food of warm character. It has no value when eaten raw because of its inherent irritating nature. But if we cook it right after it is harvested, it is good to eat because it cleans out the stomach and gets rid of bad humors. All types of nettle achieve this result."

Nettles were an important medicinal plant in medieval times and were advised for ailments such as gout, arthritis, anemia, and eczema. Applied externally, nettles were prescribed in the treatment of wounds and ulcers, as well as to stop bleeding. A tea made out of nettle was said to stimulate the circulation.

Abundant in vitamins and minerals, young nettle leaves were cooked as a vegetable, added to soups and stews. They were prime ingredients in nettle dumplings, nettle pudding, nettle beer and nettle wine.

19

Basic Ingredients

ALMONDS
(Prunus dulcis)
ALSO KNOWN AS GREEK NUTS

In terms of the dried fruit (as opposed to fresh), Saint Hildegard is insistent about the great nutritive value of almonds: "For those who seek to improve their knowledge, have bad facial coloration or headaches, it is recommended that they eat the fruit of the almond tree frequently: it will improve their thinking abilities and give them good color."

Though almonds have many familiar modern-day uses in sweet dishes and candies and are eaten raw or roasted, medieval sufferers used the oil extracted from almonds extensively in mixtures to alleviate coughs and chest conditions, and even as a means of staving off intoxication.

CHESTNUTS
(Castanea sativa)
ALSO KNOWN AS SWEET CHESTNUT

According to Hildegard, chestnuts are especially noteworthy: "The fruit of the chestnut is useful against any weakness found in mankind. Eat it often, both before and after meals: it is food for the brain, strengthens the nerves, and helps get rid of headaches.... Chestnuts are a very warm-natured food and, because of this, possess a great many qualities as they symbolize moderation, and are also useful against all types of weakness." Hildegard recommends that a person whose brain is empty from dryness "should cook the inmost kernel of the fruit of this tree in water. Having poured off the water, he should eat it often, on an empty stomach or with a meal."

Used as food, chestnuts were roasted, boiled in the same manner as other vegetables, or used for soups, pudding, and stuffings.

Basic Ingredients

MEAT AND FISH

In the vast choice of meats, the least harmful are poultry and, in the summer months, lamb or mutton. With respect to fish, apart from whale meat, Saint Hildegard speaks mainly of the fresh-water varieties.

FOODS NOT MENTIONED ABOVE

If it is easy to make one's way through the foods which Saint Hildegard wrote about, it is much more difficult to even think about or imagine what was not mentioned. Do we exclude those things she did not address? To do so would surely lead to a misunderstanding of her teachings. On one hand, she couldn't speak about those things that weren't known in her time (certain foods like potatoes, as well as some exotic foods like bananas, coffee, pineapple, and avocados were either not known or little used). On the other hand, it is also true that some of her writings may have been lost over the centuries. In other respects, some of the terms used may be uncertain due to the translation. Faced with these problems, we have two possibilities: we can either adopt a purist behavior or attitude and consider eliminating or not using what is not mentioned directly by Saint Hildegard, or we may choose to improvise, with the possible risk of making a mistake!

To remain faithful to the spirit of the rule of Saint Benedict, we have adopted a middle-of-the-road approach in this book. In the first part of the book, we have indicated the recipes which were inspired from the writings of Saint Hildegard, without adding any foods which were not known to her. In the second part, we have added certain elements about which she did not speak, always keeping her teachings in mind and not omitting any important ingredient. This simply makes good sense! By handling it in this manner, we hope to avoid the dangers that are inherent in any doctrinaire approach: being boxed in or limited by the system itself. The spirituality of Saint Hildegard would suffer even more from the rigors

Basic Ingredients

of sectarianism than from any small error that may be made with reference to one particular ingredient or another.

We invite the readers to taste the richness and great nutritional value of Saint Hildegard's diet with an open mind, remaining tolerant of other conceptions of good health, even if they seem strange to us. Charity is one of the rules that dominates all others here. It consists of the appreciation of that which comes from other sources without being hemmed in by one method alone, to the detriment of the love and fraternity of one's neighbors. If the adoption of an excellent method of eating leads us to criticize the meals generously offered by our friends, wives, or neighbors, perhaps it is better not to make any changes and stay as we are.

CHANGING YOUR DIET

Those people who want to change their diets should respect certain safety guidelines, given by Hippocrates, which go so far as to say that a bad diet is preferable to "a better one, adopted too suddenly." Not only is it important to keep your special preferences in mind (for you and your family) but also your habits. For example, if you and your family eat a great deal of meat, it might be harmful to completely eliminate it all at once. The transition to a reduction in the consumption of meat should be progressive, taken in stages. One could start by eliminating one or two meat meals a week, replacing them with cereal grains, gradually and carefully reaching the goal of keeping two or three meat meals per weak (always keeping in mind that prepared meats, chicken, and fish are considered to be meat and not vegetables). In the meantime, the "animal sub-products" (dairy products, cheeses, eggs, honey) are of vegetable origin, even though they have been produced by means of an "animal transformation process." These may be eaten with discretion, according to our personal tolerance.

Basic Ingredients

A VEGETARIAN OR MEAT DIET

In order to satisfy all different tastes, we have separated those recipes using meat from those which do not. In this way, vegetarians may more easily locate them. Those persons who want to pursue a more vegetarian diet may do so by using this section.

SPECIAL PREPARATIONS

We have also included some of Saint Hildegard's special preparations which act as remedies, but which are essentially hygienic and dietetic preparations. They have not been modified and are presented in their original format. They are gathered together in the section entitled, "Saint Hildegard's Own Special Recipes" which begins on page 63.

EATING WITH THE NATURAL WISDOM OF THE BODY

In the spirit of Hildegard, try to make the act of eating a sacred offering of thanksgiving to God rather than an automatic "hand-to-mouth" experience. Here are some ways to accomplish that goal.

1. Eat your meals in a quiet and serene environment. Eat in an atmosphere of love and joy—the two most important accompaniments of a meal. Avoid eating in the company of a noisy or high-pitched TV program. Keep family disagreements for another time.
2. Do not eat when you are on an emotional high. Food as consolation prize or as a salve for psychic discomfort is not a good idea. The food itself becomes its own problem. Use other means to assuage the pain rather than a huge slice of chocolate cake or a bowl of corn chips.
3. Do not eat standing or on the run. Sit down at the table to eat. Make your meal a restful reward.

Basic Ingredients

4. Create a setting for your meal that signals harmony for mind and body. Make the environment as well as the food pleasing to the sight as well as to the taste buds. Fashion a simple tablecloth, add fresh flowers, eat with pleasing utensils.

5. Let your appetite signal when to eat. Learn the art of either postponing your meal until you are truly hungry, or that of sitting at a meal with friends or family and not eating. Food eaten when you are already full does not satisfy.

6. Eat at a slower pace. If you cut down on distractions, such as ringing phones, newspaper stories, and TV news, you will be aware of your inner body signals and will find yourself eating once more with enjoyment. Savor the aroma of the food. Place the food in your mouth with care and ceremony. Chew with mindful attention. Experience different tastes and textures.
After you have eaten, be aware of how the food feels in your stomach and how you are feeling.

7. Eat food that is in season. Food grown locally and in season provides more of that vital energy of greenness so highly prized by Hildegard.

8. Make the end of the meal as important as the beginning. Say another prayer of thanksgiving. Even regard cleaning up as part of the process. The Vietnamese monk Thich Nhat Hanh says, "I know that if I hurry…the time of washing dishes will be unpleasant and not worth living. That would be a pity, for each minute, each second of life, is a miracle. The dishes themselves and the fact that I am here washing them are miracles!"

Basic Ingredients

HeRBS, SPiCeS, aND CONDiMeNTS

In order to ensure excellent digestion, Saint Hilde-gard recommended cooking with certain herbs and condiments. Selected spices also play an equally important role. Here, we will highlight some of the main ones used in this collection. They can gener-ally be found in grocery stores, natural food stores, or online.

"Certain plants grow from air. These plants are
gentle on the digestion and possess a happy nature,
producing happiness in anyone who eats them....
Certain other herbs are windy, since they grow
from the wind. These herbs are dry and heavy
on one's digestion. They are of a sad nature,
making the person who eats them sad...."

St. Hildegard of Bingen

Herbs That Bring Joy

DILL
(Anethum graveolens)
ALSO KNOWN AS DILLWEED

Hildegard says of dill: "Cooked, it aids digestion and suppresses numbness of the digestive process." Medieval healers used dill to make a liquid to relieve stomach cramps, sleeplessness, and headaches. Also, added to a boiled wine, dill was a remedy against hiccups.

In culinary practices, dill (fresh leaves or dried seeds) was added to vinegars, salads, stews, potato dishes, and sauces. It is still a needed ingredient in the pickling process.

GERMAN CHAMOMILE
(Mataricaria chamomilla)
ALSO SOMETIMES KNOWN AS PARIS DAISY
OR MARGUERITE

A cure-all, it is often used in combination with Roman chamomile *(Anthemis nobilis)* to which it is distantly related botanically. It may be used in the preparation of certain recipes, but its bitter taste is often not appreciated by everyone. It is preferable to sprinkle it sparingly on prepared dishes. "For a healthy person, it is good to eat as it reduces the harmful substances in the blood, increases good blood and ensures a clear head," pronounces Hildegard. She adds, "It also helps a sick person regain his strength...it aids digestion and cleans out the digestive tract. No matter how it is consumed, raw or cooked, it is good for those who are sick and for well-being in general. If it is eaten often, it may cure illness and prevent one

Herbs & Spices

from becoming ill. If it makes a person salivate, it is because it reduces bad humors and gives one good health."

HYSSOP

(Hyssopus officinalis)

We may use dried hyssop in all types of dishes, especially with meat, as it aids the digestion of same. It also may improve liver and pulmonary function. It does not lend itself as an herbal tea.

"Hyssop is, by its nature, dry and moderately warm," decrees Hildegard. "It is so strong that nothing, not even rocky soil, can prevent its growth when planted. If it is eaten often, it will make the fetid seething of the humors disappear, much like heat makes the froth of a cooking pot disappear. It is useful in all dishes. It is more useful cooked and ground into a powder. If eaten, it may help to purify the liver and clean the lungs to a certain degree. If a person has a cough and suffers from liver problems, or has reduced pulmonary function, they should eat hyssop with meat or fats and their state of health may improve. But a note of caution, if hyssop is taken alone, only with water or wine, it will do more harm than good."

Prescribed by Hippocrates, hyssop, along with rue, was recommended for asthma. Its name derives from the Greek word *azob*, or holy herb, although the hyssop of the Bible seems likely to have been a variety of marjoram. Traditionally, the purple flowers of this plant were picked separately from the leaves.

Monastics of the Middle Ages used the flowers as a tonic to keep from falling asleep during church services, and they also favored the herb to spice soups and sauces.

At one time or another, hyssop has found other uses: the vapors of a hyssop decoction were used for ear infections, the crushed leaves for cuts and bruises, and infusions of the leaves were applied externally for the pains of rheumatism.

28
—

Herbs & Spices

MINT

Mint has long been a popular herbal remedy and a mainstay in the kitchen garden. There are thought to be at least thirty species of mint and, until the seventeenth century, all mints were used in much the same way, with little attempt to differentiate between the varieties. Because of the complexity of this plant group, even botanists have difficulty determining how to name a particular specimen.

Of mint, Hildegard endorsed its use dried in cooking for its refined flavor and to aid with digestion: "Like salt, when used sparingly, it tempers foods…mint, added to meat, fish or any other food, gives it a better taste and is a good condiment; it warms the stomach and ensures good digestion."

In the Middle Ages, mint was spread around stored grain in order to keep rodents away. Monks of the time polished their teeth with fresh peppermint leaves, sprinkled mint leaves on the floors of churches in order to freshen the air, and used it to rub tabletops as a sign of hospitality.

The earliest known medical text, the Ebers Papyrus which dates from about 1550 B.C., prescribes peppermint tea as a remedy. Even today, some competitors in the Tour de France drink a combination tea of peppermint and rosemary as a stimulant.

FIELD MINT
(Mentha arvensis)
ALSO KNOWN AS WILD MINT

Whether it comes from your garden or is found growing wild, it is an excellent condiment which improves digestion. It makes an excellent herbal tea. One should take it at a different time than homeopathic preparations as it may reduce their effectiveness: "A person with a cold stomach, who has digestive problems, is advised to eat wild mint, either raw or cooked, with meat or fish, as it warms the stomach and ensures good digestion," writes Hildegard.

29

Herbs & Spices

WATER MINT

This low-growing variety of mint may aid those afflicted with pulmonary problems, in particular asthmatics, in which case it may be incorporated into all dishes in its dried form: "For those with digestive problems and who have become asthmatic, it is recommended that they eat river mint often, either raw or cooked, with meat or vegetable dishes, and the asthma may lessen because the river mint cools the fat-filled warm intestines."

POULIOT MINT

(Mentha pulegium)

ALSO KNOWN AS PENNYROYAL, PUDDING GRASS, FLEABANE

This is a variety of mint with an astonishing aroma that pleases our taste buds. Saint Hildegard, whose taste buds were, without a doubt, very subtle, recognized some fifteen different herbs in its aroma.

"Pouliot mint has a gentle warmth. When it is damp, it has some of the virtues (qualities) of the following 15 herbs: zituaire, cloves, galingale, ginger, basil, comfrey, pulmonaria (lungwort), aristolochia (birthwort or serpentaria), yarrow, southernwood (abrotanum), polypod, agrimony, stur, meadow crane's-bill, and aquatic mint. All of these plants may be helpful to reduce fever."

PARSLEY

(Petroselinum crispum)

You can sprinkle it on crudités (raw vegetables) or on prepared dishes. It is a component in the renowned "Wine for the Heart" (see page 60). Parsley is an herbal multivitamin. A cup of minced fresh parsley contains more beta carotene than a large carrot, almost twice as much vitamin C as an orange, and more calcium than a cup of milk.

Of this popular herb, Hildegard says, "Parsley is, by its nature, robust and contains more heat than cold. It grows well, thanks to the wind and humidity. It is better and more useful when it is used raw than when it is cooked. When it is eaten it may help to reduce minor fevers; however, it tends to make the spirit heavy."

In the Middle Ages, parsley was thought to prevent hair loss, so a paste was made of butter, flour, and parsley which would be rubbed on people's heads several times a year in order to preserve the strength of their hair. Parsley leaf tea was also prescribed to cure the plague, respiratory complaints, and heart pain.

Parsley, with its warm, gentle flavor, has many culinary uses—in salads, omelettes, soups, stews, and even fried or treated just as you would chopped spinach.

PSYLLIUM
(Plantago psyllium)
ALSO KNOWN AS FLEASEED, FLEAWORT, PLANTAIN

Psyllium has long been acknowledged as an important medicinal plant. Its name comes from the Greek word *psylla*, which means "flea"— a name arising from the very small seeds of the psyllium plant.

These little black seeds have remarkable absorbent properties. If you sprinkle them on foods, they permit a better intestinal passage and purify the digestive tube of all bad odors. Even today, psyllium is sometimes called a "broom for the colon."

Hildegard recommended psyllium seeds because they eliminate black bile and ensure a good cleaning of the blood. The ingestion of these seeds, however, should be accompanied by liquids so as not to cause an intestinal blockage. You can take a teaspoon in a large glass of water or any other liquid, even between meals.

Says Hildegard: "Psyllium is, by its nature, cold. But in spite of its coldness, it works to keep a tempered equilibrium. If we cook it in wine and drink this wine when it is hot, it may reduce fevers. By its tempered equilibrium, it lifts the spirit when we are down.

Herbs & Spices

As much by its coldness as by its warmness, it brings the brain back to health and gives it energy."

While the seeds have been long used as a laxative, diluted juice from the leaves has been used as a gargle for sore throats, and fresh leaves made into a poultice have been applied to bee stings.

LICORICE
(Glycyrrhiza glabra)

Licorice is an agent that softens mucus. It clarifies the voice, softens digestive mucus, and heals the membranes. However, it is contraindicated for those with high blood pressure. We can use it as an herbal tea or mix it with sweet foods: two or three good pinches. Licorice root contains an ingredient that is fifty times sweeter than sucrose. In fact, the dried licorice root can be chewed like gum.

The extract from the root, sold in sticks, is a popular candy.

For Hildegard, "Licorice is, by its nature, moderately warm. It clears the voice, no matter how we take it. It provides us with a mellow outlook, brightens the eyes, aids digestion by calming the stomach. It is, above all, most useful to those who are overstressed or hyperactive, because when it is taken frequently, it may act as a calming agent."

SAGE
(Salvia officinalis)
ALSO KNOWN AS COMMON SAGE, GARDEN SAGE, MEADOW SAGE, SCARLET SAGE

"Why should a person die of sickness while he has sage growing in his garden?" This is a saying that originated in the Middle Ages in a famous tenth-century herbal treatise. In fact, the name of this plant comes from the Latin word *sanus* meaning "healthy." Sage, traditionally associated with longevity, has a reputation for restoring a failing memory.

Herbs & Spices

The leaves of sage make an excellent herbal tea, though somewhat pungent and bitter, and useful as a digestive stimulant. This tea was also thought to "move the blood" and thus increase circulation.

Sage also has many culinary uses. It may be used in the preparation of various dishes—to cut the fatty taste of such foods as sausages, liver, and cheese dishes, to add sharpness to lighter vegetarian fare, and to pair with onion or garlic, since it stands up well to these assertive herbs.

Hildegard say that "sage, by its nature, is warm and dry. It grows better in the warmth of the sun than in humid ground. It is useful against lazy humors because it is dry. It is as good to eat raw as cooked, for it appeases those who suffer from harmful humors."

CLARY
(Salvia sclarea)
ALSO KNOWN AS CLARY SAGE

This is a popular herb native to southern Europe whose flowers have been used in medicines for eye diseases and whose seeds and foliage are used in various medicines. Hildegard says that clary sage is effective against poison, recommending it as follows: "If someone has swallowed poison, cook clary sage with a little honey or rue. After this has cooked, add a bit of apple and strain it through a cloth. This should be drunk three times, after some food, and the poison will pass through."

HART'S-TONGUE FERN
(Phyllitis scolopendrium)
The leaves of the hart's-tongue are mainly used in elixirs. This plant has remarkable properties and may prevent and cure digestive problems (liver, intestines) and pulmonary problems: "Hart's-tongue is, by its nature, warm. Its greatest value is for the liver, lungs and digestive diseases," remarks Hildegard.

33

Herbs & Spices

Spices That Bring Joy

CINNAMON
(Cinnamomum zeylanicum)

Pungent, sweet, and very hot, the powdered bark of the cinnamon tree is used in numerous desserts, giving them a pleasant aroma. Furthermore, it is a purifying and toning agent to invigorate the system and warm cold hands and feet.

"Cinnamon is, by its nature, very warm, very energetic, and contains a certain humidity, but its warmth is so strong that it eliminates the humidity," says Hildegard. "Whoever eats it will reduce bad humors and replace them with good humors."

CUMIN
(Cuminum cyminum)

A popular herb whose seeds are used to flavor food, according to Hildegard, cumin is dry and of moderate heat. She declares that "no matter how it is eaten, it is good and useful for a healthy person to eat since it furnishes a good disposition and moderates the temperature of one who is too hot."

Cumin is often used with cheese, making it more digestible. We often see it used in the Muenster and Gouda varieties. However, it is not advised for those who are ill, especially those with heart problems. Saint Hildegard advises, "If you want to eat cheese which has been cooked or baked, without digestive pain, add some cumin to it before serving."

Herbs & Spices

GALINGALE
(Alpina officinalis)
ALSO KNOWN AS LESSER GALINGALE OR CHINA ROOT

Galingale grows in Southern China, Indonesia, India, and Thailand. Galingale is a member of the ginger family, and its rhizome can be grown like that of ginger. Galingale looks similar to ginger, but for its thinner root and violet tinge.

Galingale was brought to northern Europe from the East by Crusaders and became a popular spice with its strong, hot flavor and scent somewhat reminiscent of roses. Though often used in medieval recipe books, by the eighteenth century it was used only for medicinal purposes.

Like ginger, galingale is a stimulant. It is, by its nature, warm but not hot/spicy. It works to purify the blood and its qualities as a vasodilator are good for the heart. "Galingale is totally warm, there is nothing cold in its nature, and it has many good qualities," describes Hildegard. Today, galingale is used extensively in Thai and southeast Asian cuisine; it may be purchased at Oriental grocery stores.

CLOVES
(Syzygium aromaticum)

The clove tree is native to many of the Spice Islands but is now grown in other tropical lands such as Tanzania, Jamaica, and Sri Lanka. The flower buds are a bright pinky-red and these are harvested before they open. They are then dried in the sun until they turn the familiar brown color.

This excellent spice is also a good remedy: it may purify the blood. It can be added to certain dishes in moderate quantities, mainly for those who suffer from headaches. "Cloves are extremely warm by nature, with a certain humidity which gives them gentleness, much like the moist gentleness of honey," notes Hildegard. She also recommends chewing cloves as a remedy for hiccups.

Herbs & Spices

Highly aromatic, cloves are found in many spice mixtures. They are often used to flavor apple pies. Even today, cloves are used to ease a toothache. A few cloves dry roasted in a pan will also scent and fumigate a room.

NUTMEG
(Myristica fragrans)

Nutmeg is harvested from an evergreen native to the Spice Islands and other tropical countries. Nutmeg is a popular culinary ingredient in both sweet and savory dishes. It is used in cakes, puddings, cheese or onion sauces, apple pie, stewed fruit and vegetables, especially potatoes and spinach.

Hildegard describes nutmeg as follows: "Nutmeg has a great warmth and maintains a happy equilibrium in its qualities. Those who eat it open their hearts, purify their senses, and derive a good disposition from it."

PEPPER
(Piper nigrum)

Pepper is harvested from a trailing plant native to the East Indies. Its fruits change color from red to green to black. Black pepper is made from the whole fruit, while white pepper is made from the fruit shorn of its external coat.

Pepper should be consumed in moderation, especially by those suffering from respiratory tract infections and illnesses: "Pepper is clearly warm and dry by nature," says Hildegard. "It contains an effervescent strength. If eaten in too great quantities, it is harmful, may provoke pleurisy, destroy all inherent humors, and may give rise to the production of bad humors." The Good Abbess recommends pepper as an antidote to unwillingness to eat. She advises, for this condition, the taking of a moderate amount of pepper in any food, with bread.

Herbs & Spices

Other Foods, Herbs, and Spices in Hildegard's Kitchen and Apothecary

ANGELICA
(Angelica archangelica)

Hildegard and other medieval herbalists thought angelica useful as a tonic and as a remedy for coughs and colds. Angelica, especially its green stems, is sometimes candied and used for decorating various sweet confections. The young leaves and shoots were also used in salads and poached with rhubarb to reduce the tartness of the fruit.

Crystallized angelica has long been used as decoration on cakes and desserts. To make crystallized angelica, separate the leaves and stems of about 1 pound of herb. Make a sugar syrup with 1 1/4 cups water to 1 cup sugar by boiling together. Pour the boiling syrup over the angelica to cover. Let stand for at least 24 hours. Next transfer the angelica in its syrup to a saucepan and bring to a boil. Simmer until the leaves and stems turn bright green. Drain and cool completely, then coat with superfine sugar.

37

Herbs & Spices

ANISE

(Pimpinella anisum)

Anise is an annual with feathery leaves, white flowers and, later, aromatic brown seeds. Anise has been used medicinally as far back as 1500 B.C.

Aniseed works on the digestive system and also helps respiratory ailments. Tea, made from crushed aniseeds, is said to allay colds, relieve a gassy stomach, brighten the eyes, and make the breath sweeter. A little aniseed tea mixed with warm milk and honey helps soothe a fretful child.

APPLE

(Malus pamila)

A fruit tree that Hildegard says is hot and of great moisture. The fruit is gentle and easily digested and, eaten raw, does not harm healthy people. Apples, according to the abbess, "grow from dew when it is strong. They are good for healthy people to eat raw, since they are ripened by the strong dew."

BASIL

(Ocimum basilicum)

A highly perfumed herb used often with tomatoes, eggplant, and spinach, it also gives a lift to salads, cucumbers, and pasta dishes. Basil has long been an herbal remedy and is often mixed with borage for a tonic tea to revive lowered vitality.

Basil is classified as cold by Hildegard. She recommends cooking basil in wine with honey added to make a curative for fevers.

Herbs & Spices

CELERY

(Apium graveolens)

A difficult-to-grow plant of the carrot family with thick, furrowed stalks. Hildegard declares it hot and more of a green nature than a dry one. She recommends eating it cooked rather than raw.

CHERVIL

(Anthriscus cerefolium)

A herb that resembles parsley, although its fernlike leaves are smaller and finer, and their flavor has a mild taste of aniseed. Chervil soup has often been a traditional fare for Holy Thursday.

According to Hildegard, chervil is of a "dry nature and grows from neither strong air nor the strong moisture of the earth, but arises in weak breezes, before the fertile heat of summer. It is more hot than cold, and that heat is healthful."

CHICKPEAS

ALSO KNOWN AS GARBANZO BEANS

Hildegard characterizes chickpeas as hot and gentle. They are light and easy to eat and do not increase bad humors in the person who eats them.

DANDELION

(Taraxacum officinale)

A weed that is sometimes grown in the garden and harvested early when the leaves will be less bitter. All parts of the dandelion are edible. The flowers make a pleasant tea and wine. The root can be steamed, broiled, roasted, and also toasted for coffee. Of the dandelion, Hildegard says that it is hot and moist and, in its nature, it tends toward "comeliness and it literally springs up from the earth."

DITTANY

(Origanum dictamnus)

ALSO KNOWN AS DITTANY OF CRETE, FRAXINELLA

A species of oregano that grows in low, spreading mounds and makes a delightful hanging basket. The Greeks used dittany or oregano extensively, both internally and externally. An infusion of leaves taken as tea is recommended as a spring tonic.

Hildegard classifies dittany as hot and dry and having the powers of fire and stone. She says: "Just as a stone is hard and holds heat when it comes out of a fire, so dittany is powerful against illnesses in which these qualities prevail. If a stone is beginning to grow in a person who is heavy by nature, he should pulverize dittany, and frequently eat this powder with wheat bread. It will keep the stone from growing."

FENUGREEK
(Trigonella foenum-graecum)
ALSO KNOWN AS BIRD'S FOOT, GREEK HAYSEED

An annual herb with oblong leaves and yellowish-white flowers followed by legumelike fruits containing small golden-brown seeds, fenugreek is one of the oldest cultivated plants, having been mentioned in medical papyri found in ancient Egyptian tombs. Charlemagne encouraged its cultivation in central Europe in the ninth century.

Hildegard says that fenugreek is more cold than hot. She advises its use for a person with fevers, since fenugreek brings forth frequent sweats. For those bothered by food, it is useful to take the fenugreek plant and warm its seed in wine. If this liquid is drunk warm, on an empty stomach, the patient will find himself better.

GARDEN SPURGE
(Euphorbia)

Euphorbia is a diverse group of plants distinguished by highly colored bracts, absence of petals, and a milky sap which in some cases is poisonous.

Hildegard says that garden spurge is cold and that the little sap it has is sharp. She warns that by itself it is not good for humans. "Eaten pure, mixed with nothing else, it would diffuse through a person's body and pass through unhealthfully." But spurge can be combined with other ingredients to make a gentle purgative.

Herbs & Spices

GARLIC
(Allium sativum)

A tall plant arising from a bulb covered with papery white skin and made up of parts, or cloves. Garlic is indispensable in many types of cooking and also has remarkable medicinal properties. People were bidden to eat garlic to cleanse the intestines, to lower high blood pressure, to expel worms, to ward off colds, and to alleviate rheumatism. The raw juice was put on sterilized swabs during World War I and applied to wounds.

Hildegard says that garlic has "proper heat and has its liveliness from the vigor of the dew, from the first sleep of night until daybreak nearly arrives in the morning. For sick as well as healthy people, garlic is more healthful to eat than leeks."

GENTIAN
(Gentiana lutea)
ALSO KNOWN AS YELLOW GENTIAN

A perennial with yellow-veined or spotted flowers. For Hildegard, yellow gentian is hot. For one who suffers heart pain, she recommends pulverizing yellow gentian and eating the powder in broth. A person with a stomach fever should drink this same powder in warm wine.

HAZEL
(Corylus cornuta)

A common shrub or nut-bearing tree whose fruits are small and sweet. The hazel tree, says Hildegard, "is more cold than hot." Hazelnuts are not harmful to healthy persons.

Herbs & Spices

HELLEBORE
(Helleborus niger)
ALSO KNOWN AS BLACK HELLEBORE, CHRISTMAS ROSE

An evergreen perennial with white flowers tinged with rose. It is known as the Christmas Rose because, if planted in a sheltered location close to the foundation of a building, it may even bloom in late December. Hellebore is hot and dry, according to Hildegard. "It contains a bit of moisture and a certain vital energy which is useful," she maintains.

HYSSOP
(Hyssopus officinalis)

A plant, belonging to the mint family, with narrow green leaves and deep purple flowers. Its leaves have a musky aroma and an interesting flavor of Angostura bitters. Hyssop leaves are sometimes added to the stuffings for duck, pork, and goose to diminish fattiness.

Hyssop has long been used for medicinal applications, prescribed among other things as a sedative and as a gargle for sore throats.

Hyssop is of a dry nature and is moderately hot in Hildegard's classification scheme. She says: "Eaten often, it purges the weak and stinking foam of humors; it is useful in all foods. It is more beneficial pulverized and cooked rather than raw."

JUNIPER
(Juniperus communis)

A small evergreen tree which gives off dark blue berries used to flavor gin and as a seasoning for game and other meats. Eaten as a digestive aid, the vapors arising from a tea made from its leaves or berries is inhaled to relieve colds or bronchitis. Hildegard classifies the juniper as more hot than cold.

Herbs & Spices

LAUREL

(Laurus nobilis)

ALSO KNOWN AS THE BAY LAUREL,
SWEET BAY, ROMAN LAUREL

A tree valued for its aromatic leaves which have long been used in many different types of cooking—especially as part of a savory herb bouquet known as a "bouquet garni."

Bay has many preservative and antiseptic qualities. Externally, the oil from the bay leaves and berries was applied to bruises and sprains. The smoke from burning bay leaves was believed to protect against infection. For this reason, bay had the reputation of protecting against the plague, evil, and lightning.

Hildegard characterizes the bay laurel as hot with a bit of dryness. The laurel has long symbolized constancy.

LAVENDER

(Lavendula angustifolia)

ALSO KNOWN AS ENGLISH LAVENDER

A bushy small shrub with silvery, pointed leaves and highly perfumed mauve flowers. "Lavender is hot and dry, having very little moisture," says Hildegard. "If a person with lice frequently smells lavender, the lice will die. Its odor clears the eyes and curbs very many evil things." Lavender is sometimes referred to as the "breath of angels."

LUNGWORT

(Pulmonaria angustifolia)

ALSO KNOWN AS COWSLIP

Lungwort is categorized as cold and a bit dry and not of much use except for one whose lung is swollen so that he coughs and can hardly breathe. In this case, cook lungwort in wine and drink it frequently on an empty stomach, advises Hildegard.

Herbs & Spices

MOUSE-EAR

(Cerastium vulgatum)

ALSO KNOWN AS CHICKWEED

A low-growing herb or weed with very small white flowers. "Mouse-ear," declares Hildegard, "is cold. When eaten, it strengthens the heart and reduces bad humors that have gathered in one spot. A person should not eat it by itself, for it is too harsh."

MUGWORT

(Artemisia vulgaris)

A perennial with grayish flowers and fragrant aroma. Mugwort has traditionally been an important herb in Europe, used to flavor and clarify beer, and also by crystal gazers since its leaves usually turned to the north. Mugwort, along with rue and tansy, are the historically bitter herbs eaten on Easter in memory of those eaten at Passover.

Hildegard characterizes mugwort as very hot with its juice being of great value. She says thus: "If it is cooked and eaten as a purée, it heals ailing intestines and warms a cold stomach."

OREGANO

(Origanum vulgare)

ALSO KNOWN AS WILD MARJORAM

A perennial herb with aromatic leaves and a staple plant in the herb garden. It is a popular ingredient in many cuisines and is used in pastas, pizzas, tomato dishes, sauces, and dressings. Hildegard says oregano is both hot and dry, but neither quality is strong. She reserves its use to treat fevers.

PEACH

(Prunus persica)

Hildegard regards the peach tree as more hot than cold and says that the sap of the tree is more useful as a medicine than the fruit. She pronounces the fruit of the peach tree as not particularly good for

44

Herbs & Spices

a sick person to eat. She tells anyone who wants to eat this fruit to throw away the outer skin and pit and place the rest in wine with salt and a bit of pepper.

PEAR
(Pyrus communis)

A tree whose fruit was probably eaten by Stone Age peoples. The pear tree is more cold than hot and is powerful and strong, according to Hildegard. Its fruit is also powerful, heavy, and harsh. Anyone who wishes to eat pears, advises Hildegard, should place them in water and roast them on a fire. Boiled pears are better to eat than those which are roasted since the warm water gradually cooks out their harmful sap.

PLANTAIN
(Plantago family)

A perennial, often considered a weed, whose flower and fruiting heads are small and triangular and borne at the end of a long flower stalk.

According to Hildegard's nutritional scheme, she recommends plantain leaves for ailments such as gout, arthritis, and sciatica, and gives these instructions: "Take plantain and express its juice. Give it, strained through a cloth and mixed with wine or honey, as a drink." She also recommends plantain juice as first aid for spider bites. (See pages 31–32.)

SAVORY
(Satureja hortensis)
ALSO KNOWN AS SUMMER SAVORY

An annual herb with narrow green leaves and a few small white or lilac flowers on top. The leaves and stems have a pleasant mild flavor and aroma. Dried savory leaves go into all kinds of cooked beans or into bread coatings for fish or meat.

Herbs & Spices

Summer savory has strongly beneficial properties and is often recommended as an herb to help purify the system.

Savory is hot and moderately moist, declares Hildegard. She notes that "there is something bitter in it which does not bite a person's insides but makes him well. If one with a sad mind eats it, it will make him joyful." Indeed, when it is eaten, it brightens and heals the eyes.

TURNIP
(Brassicao rapa)

A root vegetable that Hildegard declares more hot than cold. She says that although it is heavy in a person's stomach, it is easily digested. She cautions anyone who wishes to eat a turnip raw to be sure to take off the whole exterior rind.

VIOLETS
(Viola odorate)
ALSO KNOWN AS SWEET VIOLET

A hardy perennial, long treasured for the sweet fragrance of its flowers which are considered edible. Violets can be added to salads or candied to decorate cakes and other desserts. Tea from the leaves and flowers has long been used in Europe as a mild soother for asthma and heart palpitations.

Hildegard characterizes violets as a plant that is "between hot and cold. Although it is cold, it grows from the mild air which after winter is beginning to warm up."

WATERCRESS
(Nasturtium officinale)

A perennial with crisp, succulent leaves often added to salads, sandwiches, and soups. Hildegard declares watercress to be of a hot nature, and not harmful to a person in any way.

Herbs & Spices

BeVeRaGeS

Beverages in Saint Hildegard's monastery were probably limited to water, milk (from cows, goats, and sheep), wine, and beer. Drinks, as well as foods, were thought to have both medicinal and culinary uses, as do the elixirs, tonics, and soothers given in this section.

Wines and wine vinegars were other essentials in Saint Hildegard's array of curative potions. Sometimes the wine was infused with ashes, cooked with herbs, spiced, used to temper unhealthful aspects of plants, or infused with honey and herbs. This section also contains some of Hildegard's wine-based remedies.

Recommendations for herbal teas and a coffee substitute are also included here.

St. Hildegard of Bingen
believed that all should drink with health in mind.
She considered beer, spelt, coffee,
fruit juice thinned with mountain spring water,
fennel, rose hip or sage teas, wine, and
goat milk, all acceptable drinks.

Elixirs and Tonics

LAVENDER ELIXIR

2/3 cup fresh lavender flowers
3 quarts white or red wine
1 2/3 cups honey

When the lavender is freshly harvested, crush the flowers and pass through a sieve. Cook the wine with the honey at medium temperature; add to this the crushed lavender until the taste of the lavender permeates the mixture. Strain the mixture. Then, every three days (not daily), drink this lukewarm liquid. It may help alleviate pain in the liver and in the lungs. According to Hildegard, lavender wine will provide a person with pure knowledge and a clear understanding.

 Elixirs are healing remedies; they address situations of imbalance and symptoms of illness.

ELIXIR FOR THE STOMACH

1 part fresh or powdered ginger
1/2 part thyme leaf
2 parts fresh or powdered galingale
wine

Make a mixture using the proportions given above. Take 2 to 4 pinches of this mixture and add it to 1/2 glass of wine, sweetened or unsweetened. Take this elixir before going to bed for a period of 2 to 4 months.

Beverages

CLARY ELIXIR

3 tbsps clary sage leaves
1 tbsp Pouliot mint, or pennyroyal
1 tsp fennel seeds
4 cups wine
3 tbsps honey

"If the stomach is so weak that food makes it sore, take a mixture using the above proportions. Cook this in wine, adding a little honey. Strain the elixir through a cheesecloth. Drink this elixir after supper in the evening. This may help stomach problems and a return of the appetite," advises Hildegard.

The clary elixir is the most important remedy for the stomach mucous membranes, particularly in the case of a lack of acidity and loss of appetite.

Note: Large quantities of sage should not be taken during pregnancy.

The measurements of herbs in these recipes are called parts. A part can be an ounce, a gram, a tablespoon—how much a part is, is up to you. The important thing is that the same relative amounts or same method of measurement is used for all the ingredients in a particular recipe. Experiment with the amount in these recipes until you arrive at a drink that suits your tastes.

Beverages

HART'S-TONGUE ELIXIR

1 cup hart's-tongue ferns
3 cups wine
2 tbsps honey
1 tsp ground pepper
2 tsps cinnamon

Boil the hart's-tongue and wine together. Add the honey and continue to cook, then add the pepper and cinnamon and continue to cook another 1 to 2 minutes.

Strain this mixture and drink a liqueur (cordial) glass of this after every meal, as a curative for 4 to 6 weeks.

"Hart's-tongue is warm by nature and soothes the liver, lungs, and painful intestines. To use hart's-tongue, you must boil it in wine, add honey and continue to cook," directs Hildegard.

"Grind the pepper, adding double the quantity of cinnamon as pepper, cooking it a third time with the wine. Strain the mixture through a cheesecloth to make a clear beverage which you may drink before and after meals. This clear beverage may help the liver, purify the lungs, ease intestinal pain; it may help to eliminate decay and mucus (phlegm) of the internal organs of the body."

This elixir is known for its superior qualities, possibly assisting certain cases of asthma which have been resistant to other types of therapies.

 Harvest fresh, tender hart's-tongue fern from unpolluted areas.

VIOLET ELIXIR

1 tbsp violets (fresh or dried)
4 cups wine
1 tsp galingale
1 tsp powdered licorice

Cook the violets in the wine for 5 minutes. Add the galingale and licorice and cook for another 5 minutes. Strain the mixture.

"Whoever loses their appetite due to melancholy and worry, and also has soreness in the lungs, may be helped by drinking this clear beverage. It may help to reduce the melancholy, making them happy and may help heal the lungs," advises Hildegard. She further directs a person to drink a half cup of this elixir, once a day, for 4 to 6 weeks, stop for a period of time, and only start to drink it again if necessary.

Powdered licorice can be made from licorice sticks ground in a spice grinder. You may wish to make a supply all at once since many recipes in this book call for powdered licorice.

"For some people heart pain can be
a warning to reflect on their emotions and
their beliefs, or to completely change
their way of life. Whenever you feel pain
in your heart, spleen, or side,
parsley-honey wine is a great help."

St. Hildegard of Bingen

Beverages

REVITALIZING ELIXIR

1/2 cup fennel seeds
1 tbsp mouse-ear
1/4 cup galingale, grated
2 tbsps dittany or oregano
warm wine

Using the above proportions, pulverize the herb mixture and pass it through a strainer. Add 1 teaspoon of this mixture to warm (but not hot) wine and drink it 30 minutes after the meal.

"This powder maintains already existent good health and may strengthen the person who is ill, helping good digestion and giving strength. It also may help one to have good facial color. It is generally good for everybody, either the healthy or the ill, if it is taken after the meal," says Hildegard.

 Mouse-ear should not be taken by itself, for it is too harsh, advised Hildegard. But in combination with the above recipe it strengthens the heart and diminishes the bad humors which have gathered in one spot.

LEMON BALM SOOTHER

Take 1 part lemon balm to 3 parts fennel leaves, boil together in water, strain out the plants, and drink the remaining liquid. This is an elixir used to combat mental confusion. Lemon balm reduces the effects of harmful humors and prevents them from gaining the upper hand, says Hildegard. The juice from the fennel plant puts the person in a proper, cheerful mood.

Beverages

WINTER RESTORATIVE

5 cinnamon sticks, broken in half
1/2 tsp cardamom seeds
2 tbsps freshly grated ginger root
1/2 tsp whole cloves
4 cups water

Combine the spices with the water and simmer. Strain, and add honey if desired. Drink hot or iced.

BOOSTER TONIC

1 tbsp freshly ground ginger root
1 tbsp dried lavender flowers, crumbled
3 cups boiling water
juice from 1 lemon
2 tbsps honey or more to taste
1/8 tsp cayenne pepper

Combine the lavender flowers and ginger. Add the water and let steep for 10 minutes. Add the lemon juice, honey, and cayenne pepper. Strain and drink.

WARMING TONIC

1 tbsp peppermint or spearmint leaves
1 tbsp tender strawberry leaves
3 cups boiling water

Combine the leaves and steep in boiling water. Strain and drink to improve overall circulation.

Beverages

SEDATIVE TEA

1 tbsp lemon balm leaves, chopped
1 tbsp grated orange peel
1 tbsp dried marjoram
2 cups boiling water

Mix with boiling water, strain, and drink.

MINT TISANE

1 tbsp German chamomile flowers
1 tbsp lemon balm leaves, chopped
2 tbsps peppermint or spearmint
1 tbsp fennel seeds
4 cups boiling water

Mix all ingredients and infuse in boiling water. Strain and sip slowly.

 Tisane *is a French word for an herbal tea.*

Wines

Wines and wine vinegars were an essential ingredient in Saint Hildegard's array of medicinal potions. Sometimes the wine was infused with ashes, cooked with herbs, spiced, and used to temper unhealthful aspects of plants, or it was infused with honey and herbs. Here are some of Hildegard's wine-based remedies.

LEMON-FLAVORED WINE

"For the person who suffers from daily fevers, cook the leaves of the lemon tree with wine. Drink this often and he may see a reduction in the fevers. The fruit of this tree should also be eaten, as it is known to reduce fever."

HELLEBORE-FLAVORED WINE
(Christmas Rose)

"If a person suffers from the burning of the stomach, warm some hellebore and wine together. Drink this mixture when it is hot and the burning will improve."

GENTIAN-FLAVORED WINE
(Bitters)

gentian powder, to taste
red or dry white wine, warmed

"If the person who has a febrile stomach drinks a mixture of gentian powder and warm wine, their stomach will be cleaned of all the fever."

The secretion of gastric juices is stimulated at the beginning of the meal by the bitter component of the gentian. This wine mixture should be taken before meals so that the stimulating action of the gentian has already energized the stomach, intestines, and liver when eating begins. The comfort of the bitter remedy, like the spicy substances found in galingale, begin beforehand (through the tongue) before penetrating to the stomach.

GENTIAN WINE

1/2 cup spirits (or brandy)
2 tsps gentian root
1 slice each of orange and lemon warmed to taste
1/2 cup brown sugar
2 cups red or dry white wine

Soak the gentian root in the spirits for 4 hours. Add the lemon and orange slices and the brown sugar. Pour this mixture into a wine bottle and add enough wine to fill the bottle and cork it. Leave this mixture for 3 or 4 days or longer, if desired.

Beverages

CURLY MINT WINE

1 to 2 tsps curly mint juice or mint extract
1/2 glass of wine

"Drink this wine on an empty stomach before breakfast or any other meal. Mix in the quantities as above," says Hildegard.

This practice may help one overcome stiffness in rheumatic joints. For each new episode, drink this wine before meals for a few days, until an improvement is noted. Once an improvement is seen, stop drinking the wine as long as its effects are maintained.

BAY LAUREL WINE

"When one has stomach pains, cook the bay laurel in wine and drink this mixture while it is hot. It may help to rid the stomach of the mucus present, as it works to purify and reduce the fevers there," says Hildegard. Drink one half glass of this mixture twice daily.

 Important: use only bay laurel as ornamental laurel is toxic.

LAVENDER WINE

4 tsps lavender
4 cups wine

Boil the lavender (fresh or dried) for 5 or 6 minutes in the wine, filter, and pour into a sterilized wine bottle. This wine is an excellent remedy for the liver. It is good as an apéritif or as a bitter digestive (after-dinner cordial). Take a liqueur glass of this wine mixture, warmed, 2 or 3 times a day, without sweetening it.

WINE FLAVORED WITH
CRINKLED MINT

"For those who are bothered by rheumatism, press the crinkled mint in order to extract its sap (juice), strain it, add a little wine. Drink this morning and night and the rheumatism may improve," advises Hildegard.

WINE FLAVORED WITH
ROMAN MINT

Hildegard gives this prescription: "Crush the Roman mint; strain it, add a little wine; drink morning and night at bedtime. It may help gout."

PEACH WINE

**peach leaves, unsprayed by chemicals
    and thoroughly washed
pinch of powdered licorice
pepper
honey
wine**

Hildegard gives these instructions: "Especially for those with bad breath. Use peach leaves that have been taken from the tree before the fruit is ripe, crush. Add a pinch of powdered licorice, a little pepper, and enough honey to sweeten. Cook this mixture in some wine to make a clear beverage. Strain and drink this often after the noon and evening meals. This will improve bad breath and may help to rid the body and lungs of decay."

If you do not have a peach tree in your garden, use dried peach leaves from a reliable source. Mix the licorice powder, pepper, and honey to the crushed leaves. Add to boiling wine.

59

Beverages

WINE FLAVORED WITH PARSLEY, OR WINE FOR THE HEART

8 to 10 stems fresh parsley with their leaves
1 bottle (3 cups) wine
1 tbsp wine vinegar
1/3 cup to 2/3 cup honey

This is a remedy for heart and spleen problems and pains in the ribs (sides). Hildegard instructs: "Cook the parsley in the wine, add the vinegar and sufficient honey to sweeten. Cook and strain. Drink often."

Especially noted for its effects on heart weaknesses, chest pains, insomnia, and fatigue.

WINE FLAVORED WITH PULMONARIA
(Lungwort)

3 tbsps pulmonaria leaves
4 cups wine

Boil the pulmonaria leaves for 5 to 10 minutes in the wine. Strain through cheesecloth and pour into hot sterilized bottles. Drink a cordial glass of this before each meal. It may be seen to have positive effects on those who suffer from difficulty with breathing, dry cough, or choking spells. Take 2 glasses of this each day, preferably on an empty stomach.

Saint Hildegard writes that this liquid is "indicated for a person whose lungs are swollen, causing coughing and breathing problems. If drunk often on an empty stomach, a positive change may be seen."

Beverages

WINE FLAVORED WITH SAGE

4 tsps fresh or dried sage leaves
2 cups wine

Gently boil the wine and sage leaves for about 5 minutes. Drink 1 or 2 cordial glasses of this mixture 2 to 4 times a day.

Saint Hildegard prescribes this remedy for those "having problems with mucus or bad breath. After cooking sage leaves in wine and straining the mixture through a cheesecloth, drink often and the bad humors and mucus will diminish."

TEMPERED WINE

This is a simple and effective remedy for those who are quick-tempered. "When a person finds himself getting angry or sad, he should quickly warm up some wine, add a little cold water, and drink this. The result will be that the effects of those things that caused the sadness and anger will be reduced," writes Saint Hildegard.

"Whoever cooks lavender with wine,
or if the person has no wine, with honey
and water, and drinks it often lukewarm,
will alleviate the pain in the liver and
in the lungs and the steam in his chest.
Lavender wine will provide the person with
pure knowledge and a clear understanding."

St. Hildegard of Bingen

61

Beverages

Coffee and Herbal Teas

COFFEE

As a coffee substitute, you may replace regular coffee with one made from spelt. If the spelt is well roasted, it constitutes an excellent hygienic drink which eliminates black bile and revitalizes without stimulation. This beverage is particularly economical, as the grains can be reused many times. Contrary to coffee, the more it boils, the better the aroma. It is not necessary to grind the grain; reuse the mixture itself, adding 1 teaspoon with each usage.

HERBAL TEAS

A variety of simple herbal teas may be prepared as infusions in order to aid digestion or eliminate black bile, which always has a tendency to accumulate. The best-suited plants for herbal teas are lavender, violet, fennel, mint, sage, rose hip, licorice, vervain (verbena), thyme. You may also use other plants not noted above, such as anise, rosemary, linden (lime blossom), and burdock.

Beverages

SaiNT HiLDeGaRD'S oWN SPeCiaL ReCiPeS

The recipes in this section are some of Saint Hilde-
gard's own healthful creations, offered for both pre-
ventative and curative purposes. These special recipes
are still useful.

St. Hildegard of Bingen
believed in a simple eating regiment to ensure good health.

- ✂ The first meal of the day should be warm.
- ✂ Healthy people should eat later in the day.
- ✂ 2 to 3 meals per day will keep the body well nourished.
- ✂ Drink at mealtimes, but not water alone— water mixed with fruits or teas are preferred.
- ✂ Take a short nap at midday to be healthy.
- ✂ Do not eat too much and make sure your food and drink is neither too warm or too cold.
- ✂ Raw foods are hard on the stomach— cook your dishes.
- ✂ Take a walk after the evening meal.

COOKIES THAT BRING JOY

12 tbsps plus 1 tsp butter
3/4 cup brown sugar
1/3 cup honey
4 egg yolks
2 1/2 cups spelt flour
1 tsp salt
2 rounded tbsps of "Spices That Bring Joy" mixture
(see note below)

Melt the butter under low heat, add the sugar, honey, and egg yolks, beating lightly. Add the flour and salt, combine gently. Refrigerate this cookie dough after mixing, for at least one hour. Remove from refrigerator. Roll out onto a floured surface, cut with a cookie cutter. Bake on a baking sheet at 400° F for 10 to 15 minutes until just golden, watching closely.

"Take one whole nutmeg, add equal amounts of cinnamon and a pinch of cloves, grind this together until it forms a fine powder; add the flour and a little water. Make small cookies and eat these often. They will reduce the bad humors, enrich the blood, and fortify the nerves," directs Hildegard.

Children may eat up to three cookies a day, adults may eat five. These cookies may help strengthen the five senses and reduce the effects of aging. They may remove hate from the heart, assure good intelligence, reduce harmful juices (secretions), and give one a joyful spirit.

Note: "Spices That Bring Joy" mixture: 1 tbsp nutmeg; 1 tbsp cinnamon; 1 tsp cloves. This may be doubled or tripled as needed.

Special Recipes

LAXATIVE GINGER COOKIES
(for constipation)

12 parts freshly grated ginger
6 parts powdered licorice
2 1/4 cups spelt flour
milk or water sufficient to make the dough adhere

Refrigerate this cookie dough for at least one hour after mixing. Remove from refrigerator and roll out onto a floured board. Cut into small circles (or whatever cookie shape you desire) and bake at 350° F for 5 to 10 minutes.

These cookies are said to bring fat levels in the blood back to normal. They are known as a universal remedy. They maintain good health and prevent illness.

"If you suffer from constipation, pulverize ginger and mix it with a small amount of alkanet, or dyer's bugloss (*Anchusa officinalis*) juice; add enough spelt flour to make a dough; shape into cookies, and bake. Eat these cookies often, either on an empty stomach or after a meal. They may reduce the sourness of the stomach and soothe."

Special Recipes

ANTI-NAUSEA COOKIES

12 parts cumin
3 parts powdered licorice
4 parts white pepper
spelt flour
water or milk
1 egg yolk

Combine the dry ingredients, add the egg yolk and water or milk, bake. Eat these cakes every day. You may also sprinkle the spice mixture itself over bread.

"For those who suffer from nausea, it is suggested that they make a mixture of spices as above in the proportions noted, grind them together, add pure spelt flour with the yolk of an egg and water, bake in a hot oven or over hot coals. Eat these cookies, or simply take the spice mixture and sprinkle it over a slice of bread. This may reduce the hot and cold gastric juices that produce intestinal nausea," writes the Good Abbess.

These cookies may be eaten prior to trips in a car, boat, or plane, as well as during other times of nausea.

67

Special Recipes

GALINGALE ELECTUARY

1 tbsp galingale
2 tbsps oregano
2 tbsps celery seed
1 tsp white pepper
honey

Mix the ingredients together well and cook slowly.

Hildegard records this recipe: "Persons suffering from chest, heart or spleen pain and who, after having a great deal of phlegm, have a cold stomach, should mix the ingredients listed above in the quantities given to make a marmalade. Cook this slowly, without bringing the mixture to a boil. This electuary should be eaten often, as well as drinking a good mild pure wine."

Take a teaspoon of this electuary 3 times a day for 2 weeks. Following this, increase the frequency to 4 to 6 times a day for 2 months, as a curative. With this mixture, one should drink a glass of a good mild wine, muscatel or Malaga wine. The galingale electuary has been proven to be effective especially with those patients who suffer from asthma and stomach problems.

Some spice merchants, including some on the list of online sources at the end of the book, sell dried galingale, whole or ground, or you can dry the fresh root yourself.

BReaKFaST

Hildegard's recommended cereal grains include spelt whose powerful character creates a "happy mind," oats which are a healthy food for people who are well, rye which gives strength, and wheat which must be cooked with the entire grain.

These grains provide wonderful choices for a nourishing breakfast. For example, instead of the usual cup of caffeinated morning coffee, why not make a delicious muesli using the cereal grains known to bring joy? If we use spelt, we can make it delicious and creamy, flavoring it as we wish. The advantage of consuming cereal grains is that we provide our bodies with "slow sugars" which are digested slowly and easily, without a "jolt." This reduces the strain on our pancreas and prevents pangs of hunger in midmorning.

According to *St. Hildegard,* the first meal of the day should be warm, "to warm the stomach." This allows the stomach to function properly throughout the day. She recommended a good meal of toasted spelt bread, spelt coffee or fennel tea, and warm, roasted spelt porridge with dried fruit.

The first meal should be taken in the morning, shortly before midday or around midday. Only the sick and weak should eat earlier, to gain strength.

She also recommended chewing fennel seeds before eating to aid the digestion and freshen the breath.

OAT OR SPELT MUESLI

oats (rolled or flakes) or spelt flakes, or both
raisins, dried apricots
grated apple or any fruit in season
almonds or hazelnuts
milk: cow, goat, or soy
honey
cinnamon

Mix all ingredients together. The oats are more easily digested if
they are either scalded or grilled first. Grilling the oats will make
them crispy.

FLAVORED CREAM OF SPELT

1 part spelt berries (whole grains)
4 1/2 parts water
sugar or honey
grated coconut
hazelnuts
raisins
cinnamon
orange blossoms

Gently simmer the spelt and water for 90 minutes in the proportion
as noted above. Keep the cooking water for this recipe only. If, after
the allotted time, the mixture has not thickened sufficiently, reduce
it, then add, while stirring, any of the ingredients noted above in
preferred amounts. Add the cinnamon, orange blossoms, or any
other flavoring you may like. Let this mixture cool. Cooked spelt
grains may be also served with meat or vegetables, seasoned to
suit that particular recipe.

 For a creamier consistency, top with cream or milk.

Breakfast

NUTTY SPELT GRANOLA

1 cup toasted spelt flakes
1 cup oat flakes (rolled)
1/2 cup chopped walnuts
1/2 cup chopped hazelnuts or filberts
1/4 tsp ground cinnamon
1/2 cup maple or other sweetened fruit syrup
1/2 cup walnut or other nut oil
1 tsp vanilla powder
6 ozs (1 cup) dried fruit of choice

Coat a large baking sheet with cooking spray and set aside. Heat the oven to 350° F. Mix all the ingredients together except the dried fruit and stir until well mixed. Spread the mix on a baking sheet, and bake for about 25 minutes, or until the mix is a dark brown. Be sure to turn the granola mixture over several times during baking. When done, remove from the oven and cool. Then add the fruit and mix thoroughly. Store in airtight containers.

Hazelnuts and filberts are used interchangeably in the United States. Filberts are slightly larger than hazelnuts and were widely consumed during the Middle Ages. They are named after an abbot named Saint Philbert, whose August feast day is celebrated at the same time that filberts ripen.

Breakfast

GARLIC NUT BUTTER

20 nuts
1 whole garlic bulb, peeled
a few drops of water
nut oil
salt, pepper to taste

Crush together the nuts and the garlic bulb, adding a few drops of water. Add a small amount of nut oil, as if making mayonnaise. Add salt and pepper. Serve on toasted spelt bread.

SPELT CINNAMON COFFEE CAKE

1/2 cup butter
2 cups brown sugar
2 cups spelt flour
1 tbsp cinnamon

Mix together with fork until crumbly. Take out 1 cup of mixture for crumb topping. Then mix together:

1 egg, well beaten
1 tsp baking soda
1 cup buttermilk

Add to dry mixture. Put in greased 9 x 15 inch pan. Sprinkle a little additional brown sugar over the dough before adding the reserved crumb mixture to the top. Bake at 400° F for 20 minutes, or until done.

Breakfast

✻
SaLaDS

In Saint Hildegard's time, people certainly ate some raw foods that we would consider as typical salad fare. The Good Abbess warns against eating fresh lettuce, however, without a dressing, since it makes "a person's brain empty." She instructs those who wish to eat lettuce to first "temper" it by suffusing it with dill, vinegar, or garlic. Here, though, are other more modern interpretations of salads, using Hildegard's nutritional principles.

St. Hildegard, in her book, *Physica,* gives a recipe for making a salad "Whence, one who wishes to eat it should first temper it with dill, vinegar, or garlic, so that these suffuse in it a short time before it is eaten. Tempered in this way, lettuce strengthens the brain and furnishes good digestion." She did not recommend salad first at mealtime. Instead, for health one should start with soup.

DANDELIONS IN VINEGAR

fresh dandelion flowers
vinegar
parsley
salt, pepper to taste

Choose medium-sized dandelion flowers. Peel away all the green around each flower. Blanch them for a few minutes, drain. When they have cooled, put them into jars, covering them with vinegar, a pinch of salt and pepper, and a branch of parsley. Leave them steep for at least 45 days and use in the place of capers.

DANDELION SALAD

Combine the following as they are available: young, tender dandelion leaves, endive, watercress, and leaf lettuce. Mix 3 1/2 tbsps olive oil with 1 tbsp wine vinegar and season with crushed garlic clove, salt, and pepper. Mix well and garnish with croutons, bacon bits, and diced hard-boiled eggs.

 Dandelion greens are rich in minerals, such as potassium and a good source of vitamin A.

HERB AND FLOWER SALAD

Choose a mix of herb leaves, such as parsley, mint, lemon balm, basil, dandelion, chives, salad burnet, chervil, and so on. Garnish with flowers, such as violets, sage, and marigolds. Prepare a creamy dressing as follows: combine 2 hard-cooked egg yolks—sieved, 1 tsp prepared mustard, 6 tbsps cream, and 1 tbsp wine vinegar. Sweeten with a touch of honey, if desired. Pour over the salad when ready to serve and toss.

77
—

Salads

LIGHT CHICKEN SALAD

1 whole chicken
water to cover
sprigs of hyssop
2 apples, peeled, cored, and cut into small chunks
2 oranges, peeled, cut into small chunks
1 stalk of celery, cut into small chunks
2/3 cup nuts, coarsely chopped
2/3 cup raisins (soaked in water, drained)
1 cup Gruyère cheese, cut into small pieces
1 small head of leaf lettuce, torn into bits
2 ozs spinach, cut into small strips
1 clove garlic, minced
mayonnaise
salt, pepper, cumin

Cook the chicken for 1 hour in water seasoned with sprigs of hyssop. Cool, remove bones and skin, cut chicken into small chunks. Add the apples, oranges, celery, raisins, nuts, and cheese. Mix with the lettuce and spinach, add the garlic. Toss the salad with sufficient mayonnaise. Season to taste. Serve cold. Serves 6.

EXOTIC SALAD

1/2 fresh pineapple, peeled and cut into small cubes or
    1 cup canned pineapple
2 apples, peeled and cut into small cubes
1 banana, sliced
1 cup heavy cream
salt, pepper, curry powder

Beat the cream until it has the consistency of a mousse or a pudding. Season to taste. Add fruit, combining all ingredients together gently. Refrigerate before serving. Serves 6.

Salads

FIDDLEHEAD FERN SALAD

30 fiddleheads
3 parts oil
1 part vinegar
garlic, parsley
salt, pepper to taste

Blanch the fiddleheads for 3 to 4 minutes, drain; rinse with cold water, drain well again. Prepare the dressing, which should be very heavily seasoned with garlic and parsley. Add salt and pepper. Pour over the fiddleheads. Serves 4.

Fiddleheads are an early stage in the development of the ostrich fern, when they attain a height of about 5 inches and resemble a tight coil. They grow in damp and woody places in New England and Nova Scotia. They are usually brought to market around Easter.

CAULIFLOWER TERRINE

2 lbs cauliflower, cooked and chopped
oil
8 eggs
2 tsps agar
1 cup heavy cream
salt, pepper, galingale to taste

Sauté the cooked cauliflower in a small amount of oil in a large frying pan. Whisk together the eggs, agar, and cream in a large bowl. Stir in the cauliflower. Add the galingale, salt, and pepper. Pour into a cake pan and cook in a bain-marie (see page 211) for 1 hour at 350° F. Serves 6.

Serve the finished terrine with the following sauce: Into a bowl of mayonnaise (see recipe on page 158), add the following ingredients which have been finely chopped: 2 pickles, 2 hard-boiled eggs, 1 tomato. Mix well.

Salads

SALAD NIÇOISE

3 cups spelt grains, cooked and cooled
3 tomatoes, peeled and cut into chunks
1 bunch radishes, julienned
2 stalks of celery, coarsely chopped
1 mild green or red pepper, coarsely chopped
1/2 cup black olives, pitted
1/2 cup green olives, pitted
2 hard-boiled eggs, chopped
2 tbsps pine nuts
2 tsps fresh basil, finely chopped
salt, pepper to taste
vinaigrette dressing
fines herbes

Assemble all ingredients. Add your favorite vinaigrette and sprinkle with the fines herbes. Serves 6.

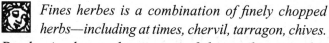 *Fines herbes is a combination of finely chopped herbes—including at times, chervil, tarragon, chives. Parsley is almost always part of the combination that makes up fines herbes.*

Salads

FENNEL TERRINE

6 fennel bulbs, trimmed and cut into halves
1 tsp dill
1 tsp galingale
coriander, salt, pepper to taste
3 tsps agar
3 eggs
3 tbsps heavy cream

Cook the fennel for 20 minutes in boiling salted water. Drain and grind in a food mill to make a purée. Season the purée with salt, pepper, coriander, dill, galingale; add the agar. Add the eggs and cream beaten together. Pour into a mold and cook for 30 to 45 minutes in a hot (400° F) oven. Remove from the mold and serve with the sauce of your choice. Serves 6.

A terrine is a layered assembly of ingredients, often containing meat, which is baked in an unlidded loaf pan and unmolded and sliced to serve.

St. Hildegard was a true believer in the powers of fennel. According to her, it is the best herb for good blood, digestion, beautiful complexion, pleasant body odor, joyfulness, and alkaline in the blood. It neutralizes black bile, removes mucus when taken in the morning on an empty stomach, and ensures good eyesight.

Salads

POULTRY LIVER TERRINE

2 cups currants
1 cup cognac
1 onion, finely chopped
oil
12 ozs (3/4 lb) poultry liver
1 cup butter
2 tbsps heavy cream
2 tsps cracked green peppercorns
1/2 tsp powdered galingale
salt, pepper to taste

Soak the currants in the cognac until plump, drain, and reserve the cognac. Brown the onions in a little oil with the liver, add the cognac (from the currants) and flambé. Make sure the chicken livers are done. Remove from heat and purée mixture in a blender. Pour into a separate bowl and add the cream, butter, green peppercorns, galingale, soaked currants, salt, and pepper. Mix well. Refrigerate for 5 to 6 hours before serving. Serves 6.

Salads

SouPS

Without a doubt, soups or potages were a dietary mainstay during Saint Hildegard's time. Here are soups featuring the traditional vegetables and seasonings. A special feature of this section is the addition of cereal grains, such as pearl barley or rice, to soups. They cook quickly and give the soup a rich consistency and better presentation. By adding cereal grains, you will also have a more nourishing dish which is easily digested. It is also possible to incorporate either spelt or oat flakes, depending upon your personal taste or preference. Cereal flakes are the product of grain preparation by which the grain is passed through metal rollers to flatten it after which it is cut into smaller flakes. Flaked cereal grains are also sometimes called rolled.

"The soul is a breath of living spirit,
that with excellent sensitivity,
permeates the entire body to give it life.
Just so, the breath of the air makes the earth fruitful.
Thus the air is the soul of the earth,
moistening it, greening it."

St. Hildegard of Bingen

HERBED CROUTONS

8 slices French or hearty whole-grain bread
2 tbsps vegetable oil
1 tbsp garlic salt, or more to taste
1/4 tsp pepper
1 tbsp dried parsley
1 tsp dried oregano
1 tsp dried basil
pinch ground thyme
1/4 tsp paprika
1/4 cup Parmesan cheese, grated

Brush each side of the bread with vegetable oil, and cut the slices into cubes. Spread the cubes in a single layer on a baking sheet lightly coated with vegetable oil. Sprinkle with the garlic salt and pepper. Bake for 12 to 15 minutes in a 350° F oven until toasted.

In the meantime, combine basil, parsley, oregano, thyme, paprika, and Parmesan in a small bowl. Sprinkle on the toasted croutons and return to oven for 2 or 3 minutes. Cool on a rack or on paper towels.

CREAMY ZUCCHINI SOUP

2 lbs zucchini, unpeeled and thickly sliced
3 tbsps oil
4 cups water
1 tbsp heavy cream
mint leaves for garnish
galingale, salt, pepper to taste

Sauté the zucchini slices in the oil. Season with the galingale, salt, and pepper. Add the water and cook for about 15 minutes. Purée the mixture in a blender or food processor. Return to pot and heat gently. When ready to serve, add the cream and garnish with the mint leaves.

85

Soups

SAINT HILDEGARD'S COUSINAT SOUP

1 lb peeled chestnuts
1/2 lb potatoes (2 medium), peeled and julienned
1/4 lb carrots (2 medium), peeled and julienned
1 stalk of celery, julienned
10 cups water
2 tbsps oil
10 whole cloves
bay leaf
1 cup heavy cream
1 egg yolk
galingale, wild thyme, salt, pepper

Cook the chestnuts and vegetables for 1 hour in the water to which the oil, whole cloves, and bay leaf have been added. When cooked, remove the cloves and bay leaf and purée in a food mill (or food processor); add the egg yolk and cream which have been mixed together. Season to taste. Serve with croutons. Serves 6.

CREAM OF TOMATO SOUP

2 large onions, finely chopped
oil
1 lb (3 medium) tomatoes, peeled and chopped
3 carrots, chopped
1 potato, peeled and chopped
1 small can tomato sauce
herbes de Provence
parsley, salt, pepper to taste
6 cups cold water
1/4 to 1/2 cup cream

Sauté the onions in hot oil until golden. Add tomatoes, carrots, potato, tomato sauce, herbes de Provence, parsley, salt, and pepper. Cook for a few minutes; add the cold water. Continue cooking for 30 minutes. Purée the mixture. Just before serving, add the cream.

Soups

CREAM OF CELERIAC SOUP

1 whole celeriac, peeled and finely chopped
2 tbsps oil
6 cups water
1 tbsp spelt flour or more if needed
2/3 cup milk
1 tbsp sherry, Jérèz if possible
1 tbsp parsley, finely chopped
salt, pepper to taste
1 egg yolk
1/4 to 1/2 cup cream

Brown the celeriac in a little oil, add the water. Cook, uncovered, for 35 minutes. Purée mixture in a blender and return it to the stove. Add the spelt flour, which has been dissolved in the milk, and cook soup until thick. Add the parsley, sherry, salt, and pepper. Mix the egg yolk with the cream and add to the soup. Serve hot.

Celeriac, also known as celery root, is a brown knob that must be peeled before using. When choosing celeriac, pick a sound knob with plenty of weight for its size. Avoid any that look shriveled or soft.

Soups

CHESTNUT SOUP

2 lbs chestnuts, peeled
4 cups water
1 tbsp Port or Madeira wine
salt, pepper to taste

Cook the peeled chestnuts for about 45 minutes in the water. Purée the mixture in a blender and return to the heat, adding enough water to make a smooth and creamy soup. Add the salt and pepper. Before serving, add the wine.

To peel chestnuts, place them in a large saucepan, add water to cover, and bring to a boil. Boil for 5 minutes and then remove the pan from the heat. Remove from heat and take two or three chestnuts from the water at a time. Quickly peel them using a sharp knife. If the chestnuts become difficult to peel after a while, return the water to a boil. Once peeled, chestnuts will keep for several days in an airtight container in the refrigerator.

"A person whose brain is empty and dry,
and who is therefore weak in the head,
should cook chestnuts in water and
eat them often. The brain will improve and
be filled up, and the nerves will be strengthened,
and in this way the head affliction will vanish."

St. Hildegard of Bingen,
from *Physica*

Soups

SPELT SOUP

1 cup dried beans
2 1/2 cups carrots, chopped
2 1/2 cups turnip, chopped
1 qt Swiss chard leaves, trimmed and chopped
8 cups water
1 cup spelt berries (whole grains, soaked overnight)
salt, pepper to taste
1/2 tsp each of galingale or freshly grated ginger,
cumin, and wild thyme

In one pot, cook the vegetables in the water for 1 hour. In another pot, cook the spelt for 1 hour in enough water to cover. When cooked, remove the vegetables from the cooking water, save this water, and grind the vegetables in a vegetable mill. Return them to their cooking water, adding the drained spelt, salt, and pepper. Put the remaining spices into a tea ball or tie into a cheesecloth. Add to the soup. Cook for 10 minutes longer. Serve hot.

Swiss chard is a member of the beet family, and one of the mildest tasting greens in contrast to mustard and turnip greens which have a much sharper taste. Search out the freshest, greenest leaves. Don't buy any that are yellowed or discolored. Be sure to wash Swiss chard well on both sides and stem.

Soups

FENNEL SOUP

4 fennel bulbs, trimmed and chopped, leaves reserved
2 zucchini, peeled and chopped
1 green pepper, chopped
2 artichoke hearts, chopped
3 tbsps oil or more as needed
1 tbsp turmeric
2 tbsps spelt flour
6 cups water
salt, pepper to taste
1 tbsp heavy cream
anise, fennel leaves (for garnish)

Brown the chopped vegetables in the oil for a few minutes, adding the turmeric and spelt flour. Add the water, salt, and pepper. Simmer for 25 minutes. When cooked, purée the mixture. Just before serving, add the cream and sprinkle the soup with the anise and the reserved chopped fennel leaves.

CREAMY ONION SOUP

4 medium yellow onions, peeled and sliced very thin
1/3 cup butter
1 tbsp spelt or oat cereal flakes
6 cups cold water
cumin, salt, pepper to taste
croutons
1 cup Gruyère cheese, grated

Brown the onions in the butter. Add the cereal flakes, stirring constantly until the roux is lightly browned. Gradually add the water, stirring constantly. Cook for 15 minutes. Purée the mixture, add the seasonings. Just before serving, top with toast rounds about 3 to 4 inches in diameter, cover with cheese, and brown under the broiler for a few minutes.

Soups

BEAN SOUP

2 lbs (1 qt) dried beans
1 tsp fennel seed
1 large onion, chopped
1 to 2 tbsps oil
1 tbsp cereal flakes, spelt or oat
2 egg yolks
2 tbsps heavy cream
pinch of cumin
salt, pepper to taste
fresh savory leaves

Soak the beans for 24 hours. Drain, add the fennel seeds and cook until beans are soft, adding enough water to cover. When cooked, drain the beans and keep the cooking liquid. In a separate pot, sauté the onion in the oil, gradually adding the cereal flakes, combine well so that the mixture does not become crumbly. Add approximately 3 cups of the reserved liquid. Add the beans. Thicken the remaining cooking liquid with the egg yolks and cream that have been mixed together, season with the cumin, salt, and pepper. Add to bean mixture. If desired, you may purée this soup before serving. When serving, sprinkle with the fresh savory.

Soups

PEASANT SOUP
(Country-style)

....

5 onions, chopped
2 tbsps oil
1 tbsp cereal flakes, oat or spelt
4 cups water
1/2 lb (1 qt) spinach, washed and cut into strips
1/2 tsp galingale or freshly grated ginger
1/4 tsp cumin
salt, pepper to taste
spelt bread or a French baguette, thinly sliced
4 ozs (3/4 cup) or more Cantal or other
    aged white cow's milk cheese, grated
1 tbsp heavy cream

Brown the onions in the oil. Sprinkle the cereal flakes over the onions and add the water, stirring constantly. Add the spinach and cook for 20 minutes. Add the galingale, cumin, salt, and pepper. In a large soup tureen, make alternate layers of sliced bread and cheese until it is three-fourths full. Add the cream to the soup to thicken. Pour soup into the prepared tureen. Serve.

Cantal is a hard, white cow's milk cheese with a sharp taste. It is from an area in central France, and it is one of the oldest cheeses known in Europe.

Soups

COCONUT CHICKEN SOUP

6 cups coconut milk
4 chicken breasts, cooked, skinned, boned,
    and cut into small strips
2 onions, chopped
zest of 1 lemon
3 tbsps lemon juice
1 tbsp galingale or freshly grated ginger
2 tbsps fresh coriander, chopped
salt, pepper to taste

Bring the coconut milk to a boil. Add the remaining ingredients and cook uncovered for 15 minutes. Serve.

Note: This soup may also be made with half or all chicken stock.

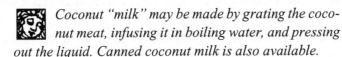 *Coconut "milk" may be made by grating the coconut meat, infusing it in boiling water, and pressing out the liquid. Canned coconut milk is also available.*

CREAMY SPRING SOUP

6 cups water
1 cup fresh nettles
1 cup plantain leaves
1/2 cup dandelion flowers (optional),
    peeled and green parts removed
pinch of powdered geranium
pinch of galingale powder
salt, pepper to taste
1/2 cup heavy cream

Cook all ingredients together for 30 minutes at low heat. Purée and add cream. Serve hot.

CREAMY HARVEST SOUP

1 cup spelt berries or kernels
3 onions, finely chopped
3 tbsps olive oil
1 1/2 lbs (4 cups) zucchini (summer squash or
    vegetable marrow), peeled and cubed
1 tsp galingale (optional)
4 cups water
1 tbsp ginger, freshly grated
salt, pepper to taste
3 egg yolks
juice of 2 lemons
mint leaves for garnish

Cook the spelt in salted water for 40 minutes, drain, and set aside. Sauté the onions in the olive oil, add the zucchini and cook for 2 minutes. Sprinkle on the galingale, if desired. Add the water and cook for approximately 30 minutes. Purée the mixture. Add the drained spelt, season with salt, pepper, and ginger.

In a separate bowl, beat the eggs with the lemon juice and a small amount of the hot soup. Add this to the hot soup, cooking gently until desired thickness is reached. When serving, garnish with fresh mint leaves.

Soups

SIMPLE HERB SOUP

2 to 3 handfuls of sorrel leaves
2 to 3 handfuls of chervil
handful of beet leaves or Swiss chard
2 to 3 handfuls of parsley leaves
3 to 4 green onions, with part of their tops
1 well-washed and trimmed head of leaf lettuce
handful of spinach leaves
1/2 cup butter
4 cups chicken stock
4 to 6 thin slices of bread, crusts removed
salt, pepper to taste

Melt the butter in a large saucepan and sauté the finely chopped herbs, lettuce, and spinach for 3 to 4 minutes. Add the stock, the slices of bread, and season with salt and pepper. Bring the soup to a gentle boil, and simmer for about 15 minutes, or until the bread disintegrates and thickens the soup.

PUMPKIN SOUP

2 lbs (5 cups) pumpkin, peeled, seeded,
and cut into large chunks
4 cups salted water
4 cups whole milk
1 tsp curry powder (or more to taste)
salt, pepper to taste

Cook the pumpkin in the salted water for 20 minutes. Drain and discard the cooking liquid. Purée the pumpkin and return it to the pot. Add the milk and heat until the mixture is creamy. Add the curry, salt, and pepper. Serve hot.

95

Soups

CREAMY FRESH BEAN SOUP

1 lb fresh navy beans (or any other legume type)
8 cups water
butter (the size of a small nut)
2 tbsps brown sugar
salt, pepper to taste
1 egg yolk, beaten

Cook the beans in the salted water until done. Drain and reserve cooking liquid. Purée cooked beans in a vegetable mill. Add the butter and 4 cups of the reserved cooking liquid. Cook for 10 minutes more, adding brown sugar. Season with salt and pepper. Just before serving, thicken with the egg yolk.

Note: Canned navy beans may be substituted in this recipe, but cooking times must be adjusted and water used in place of the cooking liquid from the beans.

Navy beans are mild, white, and oval. They are about one-fourth inch long and are sometimes confused with Great Northern beans (which are about twice the size and more kidneylike in shape). Navy beans have been fed to U.S. sailors since the 1800s, thus their distinctive name.

Soups

CeReaLS aND CeReaL GRaiNS

To St. Hildegard, the very best grain was spelt, a powerful aid to good health, and modern science has offered support for her theory, noting its ease of digestion. There are two varieties of spelt grains on the market: the small spelt grain is grown on organic farms, is very easily digested, and is flatter than the larger variety. It is preferable for consumption as a grain, but it is less desirable for bread-making. Because of its low crop yield, it costs two to three times the price of large spelt. The latter is often grown as a hybrid with wheat, which explains its lesser digestibility.

"Spelt is the best grain; it is warming,
fattening, strengthening, has a high quality,
and is milder than any other grain.
Spelt produces firm flesh and good blood,
provides a happy mind and a joyful spirit.
No matter how you eat spelt, either as a bread or
in other foods, it is good and easy to digest."

St. Hildegard of Bingen,
from *Physica*

Spelt may easily be called the survival grain of our era because of its natural resistance to all pollutants. As a result of its botanical structure, a triple seed coat, it has a built-in repulsion for all chemical fertilizers and invaders. Nutritional interest in this grain is quite remarkable. It is richer than wheat in amino acids and is more easily digested. Saint Hildegard even considered it, above all, to have the marvelous gift of bringing about a joyful spirit!

In this book, we present a number of recipes with spelt as a basis. Any dish made with spelt, which is very rich in protein, can replace a meat dish, and help us to eat less meat and strive towards a more vegetarian diet. Recent medical reports note that a daily serving of spelt grains may help reduce cholesterol and regulate the metabolism, especially those processes concerning the digestion of sugars.

Spelt may be consumed in a variety of forms: flakes (for breakfast or in soups), pasta, or whole grains, sometimes called spelt berries or spelt kernels. When spelt is not available, it may be replaced by rice or oats (except for sick persons), depending upon particular taste preferences. Saint Hildegard did not write about rice. Without a doubt, it corresponded with spelt in the diet of the Oriental people, and has somewhat similar nutritional properties.

HOW TO COOK SPELT GRAINS

Soak for 12 hours, or overnight, using 2 parts water to 1 part spelt grains. Remove any residue which comes to the surface of the water during the soaking time.

Drain the soaked spelt and rinse many times under running water.

Measure 1 part spelt to 1 1/2 parts boiling salted water and cook, covered, until tender. Depending upon the variety, spelt grains may take from 15 to 45 minutes to cook. When cooked, turn off the heat and leave covered to rest for 15 minutes.

Cooking variation: If the spelt grains are soaked for 24 hours, they will only take 20 minutes to cook, perhaps even less.

Cereals & Grains

SPELT ETOUFFÉE

2 onions, finely chopped
3 carrots, peeled and grated
2 tbsps oil
1 1/2 cups soaked spelt berries (whole grains)
salt, pepper to taste
1/2 tsp hyssop (Note: Use hyssop only in small quantities)
1/2 tsp cumin
pinch of cloves

Sauté the onions and carrots in the oil, browning lightly. Add the soaked spelt, a small amount of water, and the other seasonings. Cook, covered, for 45 minutes, checking frequently, adding water if necessary. Let it rest a few minutes off the heat. Pour off any remaining liquid and serve immediately as a side dish.

SPELT SALAD

1 cup spelt grains which have been soaked overnight
1 cup dried chickpeas which have been soaked overnight
3 apples, cored and cut into chunks
2/3 cup green olives, pitted
1 qt spinach, finely chopped
1 1/4 cups hazelnuts, coarsely chopped
2 cups green beans, cooked and cut into small pieces
2 carrots, grated
1/2 tsp each of galingale powder and cumin
salt, pepper to taste
vinaigrette dressing

Cook the soaked spelt grains and chickpeas for approximately 1 hour or until done, drain, and chill. Combine chilled chickpeas and spelt with the remaining ingredients and toss with your favorite vinaigrette dressing. Let sit for at least 10 minutes before serving. This salad is very nourishing and is a complete meal in itself.

Bread-Making
With Spelt

HOW TO MAKE YOUR OWN YEAST

Day 1, morning: Into a small bowl, pour 1 cup tepid spring water (winter months only) and add sufficient flour to make a dough that is neither too stiff nor soft. Some people add a pinch of salt or honey. Cover with a cloth and let rest for 24 hours.

Making your own yeast at home in this fashion assumes that there will be wild yeasts in the air. Test the first batch for the presence of these yeasts; if it does not work, add a little commercial yeast to get it started.

Day 2: Add a small amount of water and flour to the rested preparation. Do not double the volume. Keep the same consistency.

Day 3: Repeat Day 2 instructions.

Day 4: You may begin to use this yeast for your bread-making as long as it has risen and froths well.

It is important to care for the yeast culture properly. The more bread you make, the better the yeast becomes. Yeast is alive, so if you don't make bread more than once a week, you must feed the yeast starter every two days by adding flour and water and maintaining the consistency.

Store on the kitchen counter, covered. This way, you can watch its progress. Water temperatures vary with the seasons. When the weather is hot, let the water come to room temperature. When the weather is cold, warm the water slightly.

101

Cereals & Grains

How to Use Spelt Flour and Substitute for Wheat Flour

Spelt flour may be used for roux and sauces. Like wheat flour, it contains gluten, though its gluten is not as durable as that of wheat. Like whole wheat flour, spelt flour becomes rancid, so use it up quickly or keep it in the freezer. Spelt flakes should receive the same storage care as spelt flour.

If substituting spelt flour for wheat flour in a recipe, reduce the liquid by 25 percent. Do not overknead as the gluten is sensitive.

Measure spelt flour in a container that allows you to make sure that the flour is even with the rim. Do not pack the flour into the container and do not sift before measuring.

Cereals & Grains

SPELT BREAD

2 lbs spelt flour
4 cups water at room temperature
1 1/2 cups yeast (see page 111)
1 tbsp olive oil
salt (optional)
fenugreek seeds (optional)
galingale powder (optional)

Thin the yeast in some tepid water. Make a well in the center of the flour and add the thinned yeast, a little at a time, as well as the salt, oil, water, and eventually the seasonings. Knead until the mixture forms a smooth ball and all ingredients are well incorporated. Let rise for at least 2 hours, covered, in a warm place. Knead the dough for 30 minutes on a floured surface, adding flour as needed, up to 10 ounces. Shape into 2 long loaves and let rise again, covered, for 15 minutes.

Brush tops with a small amount of tepid water and bake in a pre-heated 450° F oven for 25 to 30 minutes. It is important to ensure that there is a pan of water on the lower rack of the oven while the bread is baking to prevent hardening of the crust. Remove finished bread from the oven and cool on a rack.

Cereals & Grains

SPELT MUFFINS

2 1/4 cups spelt flour
1/4 cup brown sugar
1 tbsp baking powder
1/2 tsp salt
1 1/4 cups milk
3 eggs, beaten
1 tbsp vegetable oil
1/2 cup chopped dates or raisins (optional)

Heat oven to 425° F. Grease and flour muffin tin. First, combine all the dry ingredients, then quickly add the milk, eggs, and oil; mix until moistened. Fill muffin tin two-third's full and bake for 15 minutes or until done. Add chopped dates or raisins to batter before baking, if desired.

SPELT TORTILLAS

2 cups spelt flour
1 tsp salt
1/4 cup vegetable oil
1/2 cup lukewarm water

Combine ingredients in a mixing bowl. Knead until dough adheres. Divide dough into 12 balls and roll out as thinly as possible. Cook on a hot, ungreased heavy skillet until lightly brown, about 45 seconds on each side.

Cereals & Grains

PaSTa

We are living in an age of pasta, prized for its ease of preparation and good nutrition. The most common ingredient in pasta in the West is wheat—either whole or refined—but other pastas are made from potatoes, rice flour, buckwheat, corn, and (even Saint Hildegard would approve) spelt, in many shapes and varieties. Use spelt pasta—or pasta made from Durham wheat—in the following recipes.

"Wheat is hot and rich. It is a complete food.
Flour must be made from wheat
without sifting out the bran,
or the result will be anemic."

St. Hildegard of Bingen
from *Causes and Cures*

NOODLES WITH VEGETABLES

1 tbsp butter
1 onion, finely chopped
2 carrots, thinly sliced
1 1/2 cups green beans, julienned
1 turnip, peeled, julienned
pinch each of cumin and galingale powder
1 tsp ginger, freshly grated
3/4 cup heavy cream
1/2 lb spelt or other noodles as desired
3/4 cup Gruyère cheese, grated

Sauté the onion in the butter, adding the remaining vegetables. Add the seasonings and steam until cooked, yet still crisp. When cooked, add the heavy cream, heating the mixture but not bringing it to a boil.

In the meantime, cook the noodles for 7 to 8 minutes in boiling, salted water. Drain. Combine the noodles and vegetable-cream mixture, toss lightly. Sprinkle with cheese.

SPAGHETTI WITH BASIL

4 to 8 cups fresh basil leaves
4 cloves of garlic
1 cup olive oil
1 tsp cumin
salt, pepper to taste
spaghetti
rounded 3/4 cup Gruyère cheese, grated

In a food processor or blender, purée the basil leaves, garlic, seasonings, and olive oil. Using 1/2 ounce of uncooked spaghetti per person as a guide, cook spaghetti in a large pot of boiling salted water until tender, yet still *al dente*. Drain spaghetti and sprinkle with the grated cheese. Serve with the basil-oil sauce.

107

Pasta

ITALIAN GNOCCHI

4 cups milk
7 Tbsps butter
pinch of salt and pepper
1/4 tsp nutmeg
1 1/4 cups spelt flour
2 eggs, beaten
1 1/4 cups Gruyère cheese, grated
1/4 tsp cumin
grated Parmesan cheese
butter
béchamel sauce (see page 160)

Bring the milk, butter, salt, pepper, and nutmeg to a boil. Add the flour, all at once to the boiling seasoned milk, stirring vigorously to form a thick mixture. Remove from heat. Add the eggs, Gruyère cheese, and cumin. Spread dough onto a buttered cookie sheet and cut into small circles, using a cookie cutter or small glass. Coat both sides with Parmesan cheese. Arrange in a buttered baking dish, overlapping the gnocchi. Dot with butter and bake in a 425° F oven for 10 minutes. Serve with a béchamel sauce lightly flavored with tomato.

Pasta

MeaT aND PouLTRY

No doubt the people of Saint Hildegard's time valued meat highly as part of their diet. In Physica, *Hildegard's book on health and healing, she declares that "herd animals that eat clean foods, like hay and similar fodder, and bear no more than one offspring at a time are—like good and useful plants—beneficial for people to eat."*

Healthy meats included poultry, lamb, beef, venison, and goat. "Kitchen Poisons" included eel, duck, sausage, fatty meat, and pork, according to *St. Hildegard*.

FILET OF BEEF WITH CREAM SAUCE

1 cup "Wine for the Heart" (see page 60)
1 tbsp mustard
1 tsp brown sugar
4 tbsps oil
5 medium onions, finely chopped
juice of 1 lemon
1 1/2 lbs filet of beef, cut into wide strips,
    1/2 inch thick
salt, pepper to taste
2 cups heavy cream
1/2 tsp galingale powder
1 tbsp coriander, chopped

Heat the wine, add the mustard and sugar and stir to combine. Let sit for 15 minutes. Sauté onions in 2 tbsps of the oil, add the lemon juice, and simmer for 20 to 30 minutes, stirring occasionally. Divide the meat into thirds and in another pan, quickly brown each portion, in turn, in the remaining 2 tbsps of very hot oil. Add the browned meat to the cooked onions and reheat, stirring in the thickened wine mixture, salt, and pepper. Remove from pan. Deglaze the pan with the heavy cream, add the galingale. Bring to a boil and return the meat-onion mixture to the pan. Sprinkle with the chopped coriander. Serve very hot.

Meat & Poultry

CHICKEN BROCHETTES

1 lb chicken breast, skinned, boned, and cubed
2 apples, cored and cut into cubes
1/2 cucumber, peeled and cubed
juice of 1 orange
4 tbsps fresh ginger, grated
2 tbsps oil or more, as needed
salt, pepper to taste
nut salad
honey vinaigrette

In the refrigerator, marinate the chicken overnight in a mixture made of the orange juice and grated ginger. Drain. Brown the chicken quickly in the oil. Make up the brochettes, alternating the pieces of cooked chicken, apples, and cucumber. Brush the brochettes with oil and grill until done. Serve with a nut salad, seasoned with a honey vinaigrette.

LOIN OF LAMB WITH THYME

2 lbs loin of lamb
2 tbsps oil
1/2 tsp galingale powder
salt, pepper to taste
branches of fresh thyme

Brown the lamb loin on all sides in a small amount of oil. Season with the salt, pepper, and galingale. Make a nest out of the thyme (or rosemary, if you prefer) branches and place the seasoned meat onto this nest. Cover and steam for approximately 20 minutes. Serve with zucchini au gratin.

Meat & Poultry

CHICKEN IN WINE OR *COQ AU VIN*

1 chicken, cut into pieces
1 onion, finely chopped
2 tbsps oil or more, as needed
1/2 cup cognac
2 cups "Wine for the Heart" (see page 60)
bouquet garni
1/2 tsp galingale powder
1/2 tsp savory
salt, pepper to taste
3 tbsps spelt flour

In the oil, sauté the chicken and onions in a heavy pot. When browned, remove from heat and flambé with the cognac. When flame has burned out, add the wine and seasonings. Let simmer for 1 hour or until cooked completely. If desired, add the chopped heart and gizzard. Just before serving, thicken the juices with the spelt flour.

CHICKEN BREAST STRIPS
WITH ROSEMARY

6 chicken breasts, skinned, boned, and cut into strips
2 tbsps olive oil
1 tsp rosemary leaves
1 onion, finely chopped
1 cup white wine
2/3 cup heavy cream
salt, pepper to taste

Steep the chicken breast strips and crumbled rosemary leaves in a little olive oil for 2 hours in the refrigerator. Sauté the chicken and onion in the olive oil for 3 minutes. Add the wine and simmer for 15 minutes. Just before serving, add the cream and heat gently. Add salt and pepper. Serve with cooked spelt berries (whole grains) and/or spinach.

113

Me

CRÊPES STUFFED WITH CHICKEN

2 chicken breasts
1 branch of hyssop
1 onion, finely chopped
10 ozs mushrooms, sliced
2 tbsps oil
salt, pepper to taste
juice of 1 lemon
pinch of cumin
1/2 cup cream
rounded 3/4 cup Cantal cheese or other
    aged white cow's milk cheese, grated
béchamel sauce (see page 160)
plain crêpes (see recipe page 186)

Cook the chicken breasts in 2 cups water with the hyssop. When cooked, drain, remove skin and bones; slice. Sauté the onions and mushrooms in a small amount of oil, add salt and pepper. Set aside.

While the chicken cooks, make the crêpes and béchamel sauce (you will need approximately 2 cups of sauce).

To the sliced cooked chicken add the onion-mushroom mixture, cumin, lemon juice, cream, half of the cheese and enough of the béchamel sauce to moisten. Fill the crêpes with this mixture, roll and place into an ovenproof dish. Cover filled crêpes with the remaining béchamel sauce, sprinkle with the remaining cheese. Brown in a moderate oven for 15 minutes before serving.

 Young chicken cooked in hyssop was recommended by Hildegard as a relief for sadness.

Meat & Poultry

BREADED SCALLOPS OF CHICKEN

3/4 cup fresh breadcrumbs
2 tbsps coriander
1/4 tsp ginger, grated
salt, pepper to taste
4 chicken scallops
2 to 3 tbsps honey
vegetable or olive oil
fresh lemon juice

Mix the breadcrumbs with the coriander, ginger, salt, and pepper.
Dip each scallop first into the honey, then into the seasoned crumbs.
Cook each of the breaded scallops in hot oil for 3 to 4 minutes on
each side, in a covered frying pan. Keep warm. Squeeze a bit of
fresh lemon juice over the cooked scallops before serving.

*A scallop or scallopini is a thin, flattened piece of
meat such as veal or breast of chicken. Scallops are
usually cut across the grain of the meat.*

115

Meat & Poultry

VEAL SCALLOPS

4 veal scallops
salt, pepper to taste
2 tbsps vegetable or olive oil
4 ozs blue cheese, crumbled
1/2 cup heavy cream
pinch each of cumin and galingale

Brown the scallops in oil in a frying pan. In a separate bowl, combine the cream, cheese, and seasonings. When the scallops are browned, remove from the frying pan and place in a single layer in an ovenproof dish. Cover with the cheese and cream mixture. Heat in a moderate oven (350° F) for 10 minutes.

VEAL MEDALLIONS

6 veal medallions (sliced filet of veal)
2 tbsps oil
3 tbsps butter
salt
1 tbsp Port wine
1 tbsp sherry vinegar
1 tbsp strong mustard
4 tbsps heavy cream
pinch of ground ginger or galingale
12 freeze-dried green peppercorns, cracked

Heat a little oil and butter in a frying pan and brown the veal medallions for about 4 minutes on each side. Add the salt. Remove from the pan and keep warm. Drain the pan and deglaze with the vinegar and wine and reduce to half its volume. Add the mustard, which has been thinned with a little vinegar, the cream and the galingale. Reduce again, stirring constantly. Add the cracked peppercorns. Pour sauce over the reserved warm medallions just before serving.

Meat & Poultry

CORNISH GAME HENS
WITH APPLES AND RAISINS

1 1/2 cups large raisins
1 1/2 cups Port wine
4 Cornish game hens
1 (8 ozs) package cream cheese
salt, pepper to taste
4 apples, peeled and cored
rose hip or blackberry jam

Soak the raisins in the Port wine until plump, drain, reserving wine. Combine the cream cheese and 1/2 cup of the soaked raisins. Stuff the fowl with this mixture. Fill the cored apples with the jam and remaining raisins; set aside. Lightly oil the exterior of the fowl, and sprinkle with salt and pepper. Place in a large roaster and bake in a 400° F oven. After 15 minutes, remove roaster and place the stuffed apples around the game hens. Add the reserve Port. Return to the oven and bake at 350° F for about 30 minutes, or until done, basting occasionally with the pan juices.

Meat & Poultry

SPRING STEW

3 pounds mutton or lamb
1 onion, studded with whole cloves
2 1/2 cups carrots, sliced
1 cup turnips, peeled and chopped
2 1/2 cups zucchini, julienned
1 cup canned navy beans (or any other legume type)
1 bouquet garni
1 branch of hyssop
pinch of wild thyme
1 stalk of celery, chopped
salt, pepper to taste
cooked spelt berries (whole grains) or rice

Place the mutton into a large pot and cover with 16 cups of water. Cook at a rolling boil for 90 minutes, skimming off the fat. Add the beans, vegetables, and seasonings. Simmer for another 45 minutes, watching that the stew does not come to a full boil. Serve the mutton on a bed of cooked spelt berries (or rice), garnish with the cooked vegetables. You may also season the broth with a little wine, if desired. Serves 6.

Meat & Poultry

ALMOND CHICKEN

1 whole chicken
1/2 lb ground veal
3/4 cup powdered or ground almonds
3/4 cup raisins
1/2 tsp each of powdered galingale and saffron
1 egg
salt, pepper to taste
1 onion, finely chopped
2 tbsps oil
1 cup cognac
1 cup finely chopped almonds

Mix the ground veal with the powdered almonds, half the raisins, galingale, saffron, egg, some salt and pepper. Stuff the chicken with this veal mixture.

In a deep, heavy pan, sauté the onion in a little oil and brown the chicken on all sides. Sprinkle with salt and pepper. Flambé the browned chicken with the cognac. Simmer for 45 minutes. At the end of the cooking time, add the chopped almonds and the remainder of the raisins. Simmer for another 15 minutes. Serves 6.

Meat & Poultry

ROSEMARY CHICKEN

1 whole chicken
rosemary-flavored oil
1 cup fresh breadcrumbs, soaked in a little milk
pinch of powdered galingale or ginger
salt, pepper to taste
chicken liver
1 egg yolk
bay leaf, ground
rosemary
1 tbsp butter
1 branch fresh hyssop

Steep the chicken in 4 cups of rosemary-flavored oil.

Prepare the stuffing as follows: mix the soaked breadcrumbs with the galingale, salt, and pepper; mash the chicken liver with the egg yolk, bay leaf, and some rosemary. Mix this all together and knead in the butter and hyssop.

Drain the chicken, reserving some of the perfumed oil. Stuff the chicken with the liver-bread mixture and drizzle with oil. (Be sure to discard the remaining oil as it is not safe to reuse.) Bake for 1 hour in a 350° F oven. Serves 6.

Rosemary is a member of the mint family and its green needlelike leaves have a slightly bitter taste with a piney aroma. Rosemary takes well to robust, roasted foods. A sprig of rosemary under the bed was reputed to banish evil dreams.

Meat & Poultry

STEWED CHICKEN

1 chicken, cut into pieces
2 onions, finely chopped
oil
oat or spelt flakes
2 cups white wine
bouquet garni
salt, pepper to taste
2 carrots, sliced
2 onions, cut into eighths
1/2 tsp galingale powder

Sauté the chopped onions and chicken pieces until browned in a little oil in a deep, heavy casserole. Sprinkle with the cereal flakes, add the white wine, bouquet garni, salt, pepper, carrots, and pieces of onion. Cook, covered for 1 hour. Just before the end of the cooking time, add the galingale. Serves 6.

Meat & Poultry

SAUTÉED VENISON
(Deer)

1 venison loin roast
1 onion, finely chopped
2 tbsps oil
spelt flour
2 cups good red wine
bouquet garni
1 stalk of celery, chopped
2 whole cloves
salt, pepper to taste
pinch each of wild thyme, crushed juniper berries, basil

In a deep, heavy casserole, brown the onion and venison loin in a little oil. Sprinkle with a small amount of spelt flour, add the wine, and the remaining ingredients. Simmer, covered, for 30 minutes, or until done. Serves 6.

Hildegard declares that the flesh of the deer is good for both healthy and sick people since the deer is gentle and of a healthy and clean nature.

Meat & Poultry

FiSH

"That's a fine kettle of fish" may be a saying that hearkens back to the importance of fish in the monastic diet of Hildegard's day. In her catalog of foods and their qualities, she lists the familiar perch and trout (for which recipes are included in this section), as well as whale, herring, cod, crawfish, salmon, and pike.

St. Hildegard of Bingen was very specific about "acceptable fish." Healthy fish included grayling, trout, bass, cod, pike, wels catfish, and pike perch. "Kitchen Poisons" included eel, crabs, tench, and plaice.

COURT-BOUILLON
(Stock)

4 cups water
2 cups white wine
1 medium onion, chopped into large chunks
1 carrot, sliced
1 stalk of celery
1 bouquet garni
10 peppercorns
salt to taste

Bring the water, wine, carrot, celery, onion, salt, pepper, and bouquet garni to a boil. Continue simmering until the vegetables are fully cooked.

You may use this court-bouillon alone as a clear soup, as a base for another soup, or as the cooking liquid for fish. In the latter case, you will require about 8 cups for each 1 1/2 pounds of fish.

Fish

PERCH WITH BAY LEAVES

2 medium-sized perch, cleaned and rinsed well
bay leaves
olive oil
juice of 2 lemons
fines herbes (see note below)
salt, pepper to taste

Ensure you clean the fish well as any traces of the entrails may cause an adverse reaction. Make a bed of bay leaves in the upper part of a steamer and lay the perch on it. Season with the salt and pepper. Steam the fish for 10 minutes.

Prepare a sauce as follows: add the lemon juice to the fines herbes, add olive oil to blend. Then add salt and pepper. Serve over the cooked perch. Serves 4.

Note: In this case, the fines herbes are composed of the following combination—1 tbsp each of parsley, chervil, and tarragon, all finely chopped together.

Perch is more hot than cold, says Hildegard. "It likes the day, dwells freely in the sunshine, and lives happily in clear waters. Its flesh is sound and good for healthy and sick people to eat."

126
—

Fish

FILET OF PERCH WITH BLUE CHEESE

1 lb zucchini, coarsely grated
2 tbsps butter or oil
1 tbsp heavy cream
pinch each of galingale and cumin
salt, pepper to taste
1 cup blue cheese, crumbled
4 perch filets
parchment paper or aluminum foil

Quickly blanch the grated zucchini in boiling, salted water. Immediately plunge into ice water and drain well on absorbent towels. Brown the drained zucchini in a small amount of butter or oil. Add the cream, seasonings, salt, and pepper. Let simmer for a few minutes, then add the crumbled blue cheese. Place each perch filet onto a buttered sheet of parchment paper (or aluminum foil), and cover with some of the sauce. Close each packet (papillote) tightly and place on a baking sheet. Bake the packets in a hot oven (425° F) for 15 minutes. Serve with remaining sauce. Serves 4.

Fish

MONKFISH, AMERICAN STYLE

4 monkfish fillets
spelt flour
2 tbsps oil
1/2 cup cognac
6 green onions
parsley
1 clove garlic
1 can tomato soup
1 cup white wine
2 cups court-bouillon with the cooked vegetables removed
2 tsps sugar
1 tsp anisette liqueur (Pastis or Ricard)
1 branch thyme
salt, cayenne pepper
cooked spelt

Dredge the monkfish in a little flour and brown on all sides in 1 tbsp oil. Flambé with a small amount of cognac. Keep warm. In the meantime, finely mince the green onions, parsley, and garlic together in a food processor or blender. Brown this mixture in 1 tbsp oil. Add the white wine, clear bouillon, tomato soup, sugar, liqueur, and seasonings. Cook and reduce this sauce for 15 minutes. Place the monkfish into the sauce and simmer for 10 to 15 minutes, or until done. Serve over cooked spelt. Serves 4.

Monkfish fillets are white meat usually taken from the tail of this ocean fish. It has the firmness and texture of lobster.

Fish

TROUT AMANDINE

4 trout, well cleaned
1/4 to 1/2 spelt flour
2 to 4 tbsps butter
1/2 cup heavy cream
1 tbsp Calvados or other fruit brandy
pinch of galingale
1/4 cup almonds, toasted
1 sliced lemon
salt, pepper to taste

Dust the trout lightly with spelt flour and brown in a small amount of butter. Flambé with the Calvados. Remove from pan and keep warm. Deglaze the pan with enough heavy cream to make sufficient sauce, add the galingale, salt, and pepper, simmer to allow spice to mellow. When serving, pour the sauce over the trout, sprinkle with the toasted almonds and decorate with lemon slices. Serves 4.

TROUT IN WHITE WINE

4 trout, well cleaned
1/4 to 1/2 cup spelt flour
2 to 4 tbsps butter
salt, pepper to taste
1 cup dry white wine
4 tbsps heavy cream
pinch each of saffron and galingale
1/2 cup of mixed parsley and chives (fines herbes) for garnish

Coat each trout with flour and cook in a small amount of butter for 5 minutes on each side. Season with salt and pepper. Remove from pan and place in a warm oven to finishing cooking. Deglaze the pan with white wine. Thicken wine with the cream. Season with saffron and galingale. Serve this sauce over the trout and garnish with the fines herbes. Serves 4.

129
——

Fish

TROUT IN PAPILLOTE

4 trout, well cleaned
pinch of galingale
salt, pepper to taste
juice of 1 lemon
4 mint leaves

Season the interior of each trout with a pinch of galingale, salt, and pepper. Place each in a piece of aluminum foil, topping with a little lemon juice and a mint leaf. Close each papillote, or pouch, and place on a baking sheet. Bake in a hot (400° F) oven for 10 minutes.

Variation: You may substitute tarragon leaves for the mint. In this case, place the tarragon on the inside of the trout. Serves 4.

En papillote *is French for wrapping or sealing food in parchment paper or aluminum foil in order to seal in the aroma and flavor during the cooking process.*

Fish

EGGs aND EGG DiSHeS

Chaucer's poor widow in The Canterbury Tales (*appropriately enough*, The Nun's Priest's Tale!) *had a diet of milk, brown bread, broiled bacon, and "sometimes an egg or two." So eggs, of course, were part of the medieval fare of both rich and poor. Egg yolks were sometimes mixed with wine and gently heated to make caudles, which were hearty drinks served at breakfast or before bed.*

Hildegard's recommended egg diet included only eggs from domesticated hens—and then only in moderation. She declared eggs roasted on a fire healthier than eggs cooked in water in the shells. However Hildegard felt about eggs, this section contains a sample of intriguing egg dishes.

Some 800 years ago *St. Hildegard of Bingen* wrote about spelt and eggs: "The spelt is the best of grains. It is rich and nourishing and milder than other grains. It produces a strong body and and healthy blood to those who eat it and it makes the spirit of man light and cheerful. If someone is ill boil some spelt, mix it with egg, and this will heal him like a fine ointment."

SPELT CAKE WITH CORIANDER

3/4 cup spelt flour
3 eggs
1 cup milk
1 bunch coriander leaves, finely chopped
pinch each of salt and pepper

Place the flour in a bowl, make a well in the center, and add the eggs, one at a time. Add the milk and beat until smooth. Add the seasonings. Pour the batter into a lightly buttered frying pan and, while gently stirring, cook until brown on one side. Flip with a spatula and cook the other side until browned. Serve hot. Serves 2.

 Coriander is a green herb that resembles parsley but has a tangy, more pungent taste. It is often used in Mexican cooking.

POACHED EGGS

4 cups water
2 tbsps vinegar
2 tbsps coarse salt
4 eggs
2 cups béchamel sauce (see page 160), seasoned with a pinch
each of cumin, fenugreek, and cloves and a few cracked
coriander and fennel seeds
4 pieces French bread, sliced and toasted

Bring the water, salt, and vinegar to a boil. Reduce heat so that the water is just simmering, not boiling. Crack the eggs and add, one at a time, to the water. Cook for 2 to 3 minutes. Drain the cooked eggs on absorbent paper. Trim off excess white, place each on a piece of toast, and then onto a baking sheet. Cover with the seasoned béchamel sauce and put into a moderate (350° F) oven for a few minutes before serving. Serves 2.

133

Eggs

NETTLE OMELETTE

1 cup tender, young nettle sprouts
butter
8 eggs
1 tsp galingale
salt, pepper to taste

In one frying pan, soften the nettle sprouts in a little butter. In a bowl, beat the eggs, add the seasonings, and the softened nettles. Melt 2 to 3 tbsps butter in large non-stick frying pan, pour in the egg mixture and cook gently, pushing the sides of the omelette in toward the center as they begin to cook. This way the liquid egg from the center flows to the edges and cooks. When the eggs are cooked, yet still moist, fold one half of the omelette over and quickly place it on a plate. Serves 4.

Eggs

✳ VeGeTaBLeS

Plants used as vegetables in Hildegard's cookery make up a plenteous cornucopia: cabbage, parsnips, radishes, leeks, beans, lentils, turnips, peas, onions, beets, mushrooms, squash, celery, fennel, and chestnuts. Here is a sample of healthy vegetable dishes in the Hildegard style.

St. Hildegard's recommended vegetables include beans of all types, fennel, celery, corn-on-the-cob, chickpeas, pumpkin, watercress, red beets, lettuce (only with dressing; strengthens the brain and provides good digestion), onions (cooked), broccoli, and, of course, chestnuts (fills empty brain, strengthens heart, liver, and stomach).

OLIVE CHESTNUT LOAF

1 1/2 cups spelt flour, sifted
2 tsps baking powder
pinch of salt
4 eggs
2/3 cup milk
1/3 cup oil
pinch of cumin
salt, pepper to taste
3/4 cup pitted green olives
1 1/4 cups Gruyère cheese, grated
3/4 cup chestnuts, peeled and chopped into large chunks
fresh tomato salsa (optional)

Preheat the oven to moderate (350° F). Combine the flour, baking powder, and salt, add the eggs, one at a time, beating with a wooden spoon. Continue mixing, add the oil and milk. Beat until the dough is thick and smooth. Add the cumin and salt and pepper to taste. Drain the olives and rinse under cold water, drain again. Carefully fold the olives, cheese, and chestnuts into the dough. Fill a buttered loaf pan no more than two-thirds full. Bake for 1 hour. When baked, immediately remove from pan and let cool on a rack. Slice and garnish when cool. Serve with fresh tomato salsa, if desired. Serves 6.

BRAISED CHESTNUTS

1 lb chestnuts, peeled and cored
1 tbsp butter
pinch of celery salt
salt, pepper to taste

Sauté the chestnuts in the butter. Add a small amount of water and simmer, covered, for 90 minutes, adding small amounts of water only as necessary. Add seasonings. May be served with a roasted chicken.

Vegetables

BRAISED CARROTS

1 onion, diced into large chunks
2 tbsps oil
1 lb carrots, thinly sliced
1 bouquet garni
pinch of either nutmeg or cloves (whatever you prefer)
salt, pepper to taste
1 tbsp brown sugar
1/2 cup white wine
sprig of hyssop (optional)

Sauté the onions in the oil until transparent, then add the carrots, seasonings, and sugar. Simmer for a few minutes, then add the wine and hyssop. Cover and simmer until vegetables are cooked. Serves 5.

MIXED VEGETABLES

2 cups new carrots, diced
1 cup turnips, diced
1 cup green beans, diced
2 cups fresh green peas
2 hyssop leaves
1 bouquet garni
wild thyme, salt, and pepper to taste

Bring enough salted water to cover, the bouquet garni, and seasonings to a boil. Add the carrots and turnips, cook for 5 minutes, then add the beans and peas. Watch carefully, adding more water if necessary and cooking only until just done. Drain and serve immediately. Serves 6.

Vegetables

GRILLED ZUCCHINI

3 lbs zucchini
coarse salt
olive oil
3 cloves of garlic, finely chopped
7 stalks of fresh mint
1 stem of parsley
juice of 1 lemon
pinch of powdered galingale or ginger
pepper

Wash, but do not peel zucchini. Cut into long strips, 1 inch thick. Sprinkle strips with coarse salt and let drain for 30 minutes. Sponge dry. Oil the zucchini well on both sides and cook on the barbecue grill for 2 to 3 minutes per side. In the meantime, combine the garlic, mint, and parsley. Place the grilled zucchini strips in a single layer in an ovenproof dish and spread the garlic mixture over them. Sprinkle with the lemon juice and an equal amount of olive oil, as well as the galingale and pepper. Warm in the oven. Serves 4.

Vegetables

ZUCCHINI WITH SPELT

4 zucchini, peeled and cubed
1 onion, minced
2 tbsps oil
1/2 cup cooked spelt berries (whole grains)
7 tbsps butter
pinch of galingale
1 tsp saffron
1 2/3 cups chicken stock
white wine
rounded 3/4 cup Gruyère or Parmesan cheese, grated
pinch of cumin
salt, pepper to taste

Sauté the onion and zucchini in a little oil. Put aside. Brown the cooked spelt berries in the butter; add the onions and zucchini as well as the galingale and saffron. Add enough chicken stock to cover and cook for 1 hour at low heat. Check often, adding wine as necessary to keep the mixture moistened. At the end of the cooking time, there should be little or no liquid left. Sprinkle cooked mixture with the grated cheese, cumin, salt, and pepper. Serves 5.

Vegetables

CRÊPES STUFFED WITH SWISS CHARD

3 lbs Swiss chard leaves, washed and deveined
3 tbsps oil
1 1/2 cups blue cheese or more if needed
pinch of galingale
salt, pepper to taste
2 cups béchamel sauce (see page 170)
cumin
15 crêpes (see page 196)

Cook the Swiss chard leaves in boiling water for about 10 minutes, drain, and reserve some of the cooking liquid. Brown drained leaves in the oil; add the cheese (which has been melted in a little of the cooking liquid from the Swiss chard), galingale, salt, and pepper. Fill the crêpes with this mixture, roll and place in an ovenproof dish. Cover with the béchamel sauce and a sprinkle of cumin. Place in a moderate oven (350° F) until fully warmed. Serves 7.

FENNEL IN COCONUT MILK

6 fennel bulbs, trimmed and cut in half
2 tbsps oil
2 cups coconut milk, canned or fresh
1 tsp freshly grated ginger
juice of 1 lemon
1/2 tsp coriander
salt, pepper to taste
chopped parsley for garnish
6 cups cooked spelt berries (whole grains)

In an deep casserole dish, lightly brown the fennel in the oil. Add the coconut milk, salt, pepper, ginger, coriander, and lemon juice. Cook at low heat for 30 minutes. When serving, garnish with parsley. Serve with cooked spelt grains. Serves 6.

141

Vegetables

FENNEL IN WHITE WINE

1 onion, chopped
oil
spelt flour
white wine
4 fennel bulbs, trimmed and halved
juice of 1 lemon
1 tsp each of coriander, galingale, anise, and cumin
salt, pepper to taste
1/2 cup Gruyère cheese, grated

Brown onions in oil and set aside. In the pan, combine spelt flour and white wine. Add the browned onions, fennel bulbs, seasonings, and lemon juice. Cook over a low heat for 30 minutes. If needed, add a little water during cooking. Remove mixture from pan and place in an ovenproof dish. Sprinkle with the grated cheese and brown in a hot (400° F) oven for 15 minutes. Serves 4.

SPRING BEANS

1 large onion, minced
oil
2 lbs fresh navy beans, shelled
thyme, bay leaves, parsley, fennel
salt, pepper to taste
2 cups water, or as needed
2 tbsps spelt flour
1 tbsp vinegar

Brown the onion in a little oil. Add the beans and seasonings (in quantities to suit your own personal taste). Add a little water, cover, and cook at low heat for 45 minutes, checking often, adding water as necessary. When the beans are cooked, add the flour and vinegar. Cook uncovered until beans are thickened, if necessary. Serve very hot. Serves 6.

Vegetables

NETTLE FLAN

3 eggs
2 cups milk
2 cups nettles, chopped
1 tsp agar
salt
1 tsp dill
fresh parsley for garnish

Beat the eggs with the milk. Add the nettles, agar, dill, and salt. Bake in a slow oven in a flan dish, placed in a bain-marie, for 45 minutes. Garnish with fresh parsley. Serves 3.

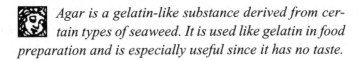 *Agar is a gelatin-like substance derived from certain types of seaweed. It is used like gelatin in food preparation and is especially useful since it has no taste.*

ARTICHOKE CUPS

4 artichokes
1 cup béchamel sauce (see page 160)
1 tbsp heavy cream
3/4 cup Cantal or other aged white cheese, grated
nutmeg, salt, pepper, galingale to taste
1/2 cup cooked fresh green peas

Cook the artichokes in salted water until the bottom can be pierced with a fork. Remove the leaves. Scrape out the choke in the center (the furry part in the heart of the artichoke). Keep the hollowed artichoke bottoms, set aside.

In a separate bowl, add the heavy cream to the béchamel sauce, as well as the cheese and seasonings. Fill the reserved artichoke cups with the peas, covering with the sauce mixture. Place in an ovenproof dish and bake in a moderate (350° F) oven for 15 minutes. Serves 4.

143

Vegetables

HERB CAKE

2 cups milk
1 1/2 cups spelt flour
5 eggs
1 onion, minced
1 cup nettles, minced
parsley, finely chopped
1/2 cup basil leaves, chopped
1/2 tsp galingale
pepper

Mix the flour and milk. Add the eggs, one at a time, beating well. Add the onion, nettles, and seasonings. Pour into a greased cake pan and bake at 350° F for 1 hour, or until done (when tested with a toothpick in the center, it comes out clean). Remove from pan. Serves 6.

NETTLE CAKE

3 cups nettles
2 tbsps butter
6 eggs, beaten
1/2 tsp each of galingale and cinnamon
pinch each of curry and nutmeg
1 cup nuts, chopped
salt, pepper to taste
2 cups béchamel sauce (see page 160)

Cook the nettles in a frying pan with a little butter until softened, set aside to cool. In a bowl, add the eggs, seasonings, and nuts to the béchamel sauce. Combine with the nettles and pour into a cake pan. Bake in a bain-marie in a moderate (350° F) oven for 45 minutes.

Vegetables

MILD CURRY

4 rounded tbsps cinnamon
4 rounded tbsps cloves
4 rounded tbsps cumin seeds
4 rounded tbsps cardamom seeds

Grind all the spices together. Store in an airtight container. You may use this mixture to season any curry dish. (See other curry recipes on pages 163–164.)

ARNAUD'S FENNEL AU GRATIN

6 fennel bulbs
2 cups béchamel sauce (see page 170)
1/2 tsp cumin
1 tsp galingale
pinch of freshly ground nutmeg
salt, pepper to taste
3/4 cup Cantal or other aged white cheese, grated

Steam the peeled fennel bulbs for 20 minutes. In a separate bowl, add the seasonings to the béchamel sauce. Place the steamed fennel in an ovenproof dish and cover with the seasoned sauce. Sprinkle with grated cheese. Bake in a moderate (350° F) oven for 20 minutes. Serves 6.

Vegetables

THOUSAND VEGETABLE CAKE

4 red peppers
3 fennel bulbs
3 stalks of celery
1 zucchini
1 cucumber
1 large onion
2 tbsps oil
1/2 cup butter
3 eggs
zest of 1 lemon
2 tsps baking powder
1 3/4 cups spelt flour
2 tbsps heavy cream
1/2 cup "Wine for the Heart" (see page 60)
1/2 tsp each of nutmeg, anise, cumin, galingale (optional)
1/2 tsp salt
pepper to taste

Dice all vegetables and sauté them in a small amount of oil until just cooked but still crisp. Set aside.

In the meantime, make the batter as follows: soften the butter; add the eggs, one at a time, beating after each addition, add the lemon zest, baking powder, and flour. Mix until smooth. Add the cream, wine, and seasonings, blending well.

Place the cooked vegetables into a cake pan of your choice, pour the batter over the vegetables. Bake in a hot (400° F) oven for 45 minutes. Serves 6.

Vegetables

SWISS CHARD LOAF

**1 1/2 cups (or more if you wish) Swiss chard leaves,
    cleaned and trimmed**
2 cups spelt flour
pinch of galingale and chopped fresh parsley
salt, pepper to taste
2 cups milk
3 eggs
1/2 cup oil

Cook the Swiss chard in boiling, salted water for 10 minutes. Drain
and chop very fine.

In the meantime, make the batter: mix the spelt flour and seasonings; add the milk, eggs, and oil, beat until smooth.

Add the Swiss chard to the batter. Pour mixture into a buttered loaf
pan and bake for 45 minutes in a moderate (350° F) oven. Serves 4.

GREEN PEAS AND BEANS

1 lb new small onions
2 tbsps oil
2 lbs fresh green peas, shelled
2 lbs fresh navy (or any other legume type) beans
1/2 cup water
2 tbsps butter
salt, pepper to taste
fresh mint leaves for garnish

Sauté the onions in the oil; add the peas and beans. Add the water,
salt, and pepper. Cook for 20 minutes at low heat. Drain and serve
with a little butter; garnish with the fresh mint. Serves 6.

147

Vegetables

FRENCH PIPERADE
(Vegetable Omelette Stuffed With Spelt)

**2 cups spelt berries (whole grains) which have been
    soaked for 24 hours**
2 tbsps oil
2 tomatoes, peeled and thinly sliced
1 green pepper, chopped
2 onions, minced
1 tbsp each of chives, tarragon, and parsley
salt, pepper to taste
6 eggs
1 tbsp butter
1/4 cup Parmesan cheese, grated

Drain the soaked spelt and sauté in half of the oil. Set aside.

Sauté the vegetables and seasonings in the remainder of the oil
until just cooked but still crisp. Set aside.

Beat the eggs. Add half to the vegetable mixture, along with 1/2
of the Parmesan cheese.

In a separate large frying pan, melt the butter and pour in the
remainder of the eggs. Cook as an omelette. When the eggs begin
to coagulate, add the egg-vegetable mixture and continue cooking
at low heat. When cooked, place the cooked spelt on 1/2 of the
omelette, fold the other half over the spelt. Sprinkle with 1/2 of the
Parmesan cheese. Serve hot. Serves 6.

148

Vegetables

CHICKPEAS WITH VEGETABLES

2 lbs chickpeas, which have been soaked overnight
bouquet garni
sprig of hyssop
1 onion, minced
2 carrots, chopped
2 1/2 cups green beans, sliced
1 fennel bulb, minced
1 zucchini, chopped
1 tsp each of cumin and wild thyme
salt, pepper to taste
1 tsp galingale
dash of vinegar
1 egg yolk, beaten

Drain the soaked chickpeas. Add enough water to cover the beans. Add the hyssop and bouquet garni; cook for 3 hours, or until done. Drain and set aside.

In the meantime, sauté the remaining vegetables, adding the cumin, thyme, salt, and pepper. Simmer, covered, for 5 minutes (or until just cooked but still crisp), adding liquid as required. Combine the cooked chickpeas, galingale, and vinegar; add a little of this liquid to the egg yolk. When thickened, return to mixture and simmer for 5 minutes. Serve very hot. Serves 6.

Vegetables

SAUTÉED VEGETABLES

2 medium carrots, thinly sliced
1 onion, minced
1 tbsp oil
2 cups green beans
1/2 fennel bulb, chopped
1/2 zucchini, julienned
hyssop (optional) or mint
salt, pepper to taste
1/4 tsp galingale

Sauté onion and carrots in a small amount of oil for about 5 minutes. Add the green beans, fennel, zucchini, hyssop or mint, salt, and pepper. Cook, covered at very low heat until done, but still crisp, checking often. Add small amount of water if needed to moisten during the cooking time (no more than 1/4 cup in total). When serving, sprinkle with the galingale. Serves 4.

SPINACH QUICHE

2 eggs
1 cup milk
salt, pepper to taste
1 lb cooked spinach
1 baked pie shell
galingale
2 tbsps chopped nuts

Beat the eggs; add the milk, salt, and pepper, beat again. Put the cooked spinach in the bottom of the baked pie shell, cover with egg mixture. Bake in a hot (400° F) oven for about 35 minutes, or until eggs are set. Serve warm with a garnish of chopped nuts and galingale. If desired, the spinach may be replaced by cooked nettles. Serves 6.

PUMPKIN QUICHE

3 cups pumpkin, peeled and cut into chunks
1 branch fresh thyme
1 bay leaf
pinch of salt
2 cups béchamel sauce (see page 160)
pinch of nutmeg
2 eggs, separated
juice of 1 lemon
1 tsp each of turmeric and cumin
1/2 tsp each of fenugreek and coriander
1/4 tsp freshly grated ginger
1 1/4 cups Gruyère cheese, grated
1 baked pie shell

Cook the pumpkin in boiling water with the thyme, bay leaf, and salt for 30 to 40 minutes. Drain and purée in a food processor. Add the béchamel sauce and nutmeg to the pumpkin purée. Add the egg yolks, lemon juice, and remaining spices. When mixed well, add the cheese.

In a separate bowl, beat the egg whites until they are stiff and carefully fold into the egg-pumpkin mixture. Pour into the baked pie shell. Bake in a hot (400° F) oven for 35 minutes. Serves 6.

Veg

TUNISIAN RATATOUILLE

2 cups onions, chopped into small pieces
2 tbsps olive oil
fines herbes
salt, pepper to taste
2 cups tomatoes, peeled and cut into small pieces
2 cups apples, peeled and cut into small pieces
few drops of Tabasco sauce

Add the seasonings to the onions and sauté in half of the olive oil over a low heat for about 5 minutes. Add the tomatoes and apples, simmer for 1 hour. When mixture is cooked, add the remaining olive oil and Tabasco sauce. Cook uncovered until all the juice has evaporated. Serve very hot. Serves 6.

Note: Traditionalists may wish to add zucchini and eggplant (which have been peeled, sliced, salted, and drained under a weighted plate for 1 hour) and thinly sliced green peppers. Add these at the same time as the tomatoes and apples.

CARROT TERRINE

10 medium carrots, chopped
zest and juice of 2 oranges
3 eggs
2/3 cup heavy cream
1 1/4 cups finely chopped nuts
1 tsp agar
1/2 tsp each of galingale and licorice powder
salt, pepper to taste

Cook the carrots in boiling water until tender. Drain and purée. Add the remaining ingredients to the purée, mixing well. Pour into a loaf pan and bake in a bain-marie (see page 211) for 1 hour in a hot (400° F) oven. Serves 8.

Serving suggestion: Serve this terrine with a cheese sauce.

FENNEL SOUFFLÉ

3 fennel bulbs, trimmed and cut in half
1 onion, minced
oil
2 cups béchamel sauce (see page 160)
4 eggs, separated
3/4 cup Gruyère cheese, grated
1/2 tsp galingale
salt, pepper to taste

Cook the fennel bulbs in boiling, salted water for 20 minutes until tender. Sauté the onion in a little oil, add the cooked fennel, and mash with a fork. Add the béchamel sauce, egg yolks, cheese, and seasonings; mixing well. Remove from heat.

In a bowl, beat the egg whites until stiff and carefully fold into the vegetable mixture. Pour into an ovenproof dish and bake for 20 minutes in a moderate (350° F) oven. Serves 6.

Vegetables

CHINESE SQUASH SOUFFLÉ

2 lbs Chinese squash (see note)
4 egg yolks
5 egg whites
1 1/4 cups Gruyère cheese, grated
2 cups béchamel sauce (see page 170)
pinch of nutmeg
1 tsp cumin
salt, pepper to taste

Cook the squash in boiling, salted water; drain and purée. Add the seasonings, egg yolks, cheese, and béchamel sauce to the purée; set aside.

In a bowl, beat the egg whites until stiff and carefully fold into the purée mixture. Pour mixture into individual ramekins and bake for 25 minutes in a moderate (350° F) oven. Serves 6.

Note: The Chinese squash used in this recipe is a type of winter squash that tastes like chestnuts. If it is unavailable in your area, you may easily substitute any winter squash of your choice.

Vegetables

SauCeS, DiPS, ViNaiGReTTeS, aND RouX

The recipes here are for some of the basics: dips for vegetables, instructions for preparing roux, sour cream, and mayonnaise, dressings for salads, a wonderful herb sauce for fish, and the all-useful béchamel or white sauce.

St. Hildegard believed that many of the leaf vegetables (lettuce, chard, etc.) should only be used with dressings. Her standard dressing consisted of one tablespoon pure wine vinegar, three tablespoons sunflower oil, and a bit of brown sugar (to compensate for the sour taste). Goat's milk yogurt and lemon juice could also be used.

DIP FOR CRUDITÉS #1
(Raw Vegetables)

1 (8 ozs) package cream cheese
juice of 1 lemon, or more if needed
1 bunch finely chopped chives
pinch of galingale
salt, pepper to taste

Beat all ingredients together. Refrigerate.

DIP FOR CRUDITÉS #2
(Raw Vegetables)

1 (8 ozs) package cream cheese
juice of 1 lemon, or more if needed
1 tsp chopped chervil
1 tsp tarragon
1 tsp chopped chives
pinch of galingale
salt, pepper to taste

Mix all ingredients together well. Refrigerate. May also be served
with a vegetable terrine.

Sauces, Dips,
Vinaigrettes,
and Roux

SAUCE FOR CUCUMBERS

1 tsp lemon juice or more if needed
1/2 tsp mustard
1/2 tsp brown sugar
3 tbsps cream cheese, softened
pinch each of galingale and dill
salt, pepper to taste

Mix all ingredients together well. Pour over thinly sliced cucumbers. Refrigerate and serve.

SOUR CREAM

1 container heavy cream
1 tsp brown sugar
1 tbsp vinegar
juice of 1 lemon
salt, pepper to taste

Warm the vinegar and dissolve the sugar in it. Add the lemon juice, salt, pepper, and cream. Mix well. Refrigerate.

MAYONNAISE

1 egg yolk
1/2 tsp mustard
1/2 tsp lemon juice (optional)
salt, pepper, galingale to taste
1 cup oil

Beat the egg yolk until creamy. Add the seasonings, mustard, and lemon juice, if desired. Add the oil, a drop at a time, beating well after each addition. Add sufficient oil just until the eggs will absorb no more. Make sure that the oil is well incorporated so that it won't separate. Refrigerate.

Sauces, Dips,
Vinaigrettes,
and Roux

VINAIGRETTE #1

1 tbsp sherry or wine vinegar
1/2 tsp honey
1/2 tsp mustard
1/2 tsp geranium powder
3 tbsps olive oil
salt, pepper to taste

Mix all ingredients together in a jar. Shake well. Refrigerate.

VINAIGRETTE #2

1 tbsp ground almonds
1 tbsp sherry or wine vinegar
2 tbsps nut oil
pinch of galingale and dill
salt, pepper to taste

Mix ingredients together well. Refrigerate.

BASIC ROUX

2 tbsps butter
2 tbsps flour

Melt the butter in a frying pan without browning it (if you want a brown roux: see note). Add the flour, mixing constantly until it has emulsified. Cook gently for a few minutes. Roux is used to thicken sauces and soups.

Note: If you want to make a brown roux, let the butter brown before you add the flour.

Sauces, Dips,
Vinaigrettes,
and Roux

GREEN SAUCE FOR FISH

**1 cup of chopped mixed herbs: tarragon, parsley,
   salad burnet, and watercress**
4 hard-boiled egg yolks
3 to 4 tbsps olive oil, or more if needed
juice of 1 lemon
pinch of nutmeg
salt, pepper to taste

Blanch the herbs; drain and rinse in cold water, drain again. Put into a mortar and pestle and mix well with the hard-boiled egg yolks or use a food processor. If necessary, strain this through a sieve to smooth out any lumps. To this herb mixture, add the olive oil, a drop at a time, in the same manner as you do to make mayonnaise, beating constantly. Add the lemon juice, nutmeg, salt, and pepper. This sauce goes well with all fish dishes.

BASIC BÉCHAMEL SAUCE

11 cups milk
10 tbsps butter
10 tbsps flour
4 tbsps minced onion (optional)
sprig of thyme
1 bay leaf
pinch of nutmeg
salt, pepper to taste

Make a white roux with the butter and flour, set aside. Bring the milk to a boil. Add the roux and seasonings, stirring constantly, until desired thickness is reached. Simmer gently, making sure not to burn the bottom of the pan. Strain through a cheesecloth. Makes 11 cups.

160

Sauces, Dips,
Vinaigrettes,
and Roux

SPiCe MiXTuReS

The spice seasoning recipes here are generally for curry dishes, but we also offer one inspired by the herbs and spices recommended by Saint Hildegard herself. These recipes are guidelines. You may vary the proportions of the ingredients according to your own personal preferences. Be creative!

St. Hildegard's Healthy Spices: water mint, mugwort, Spanish chamomile root, nettles, watercress, burning bush root, gentian root, fennel, psyllium, galangal root, raw garlic, spearmint, cubeb, lavender, lovage, fruit of the bay tree, saltbush, poppy, nutmeg, cumin, clove, parsley, polemize, wild thyme, tansy, sage, yarrow, licorice root, rue, hyssop, cinnamon.

SAINT HILDEGARD'S
SPICE MIXTURE

3 tbsps cumin seeds, toasted and ground
3 tbsps fennel seeds, toasted and ground
4 tbsps fenugreek seeds, slightly toasted and ground
1 tbsp nutmeg, ground
1 tbsp cinnamon, ground

Mix all spices together and store in an airtight container.

WEST INDIAN CURRY SEASONING

1 1/2 tbsps coriander seed
1 tbsp aniseed
1 tbsp cumin
1 tbsp fenugreek seeds
1 tbsp black pepper
1 tbsp chopped almonds
1 cinnamon stick
2 tbsps ground ginger
2 tbsps ground turmeric

Heat the spices in a dry frying pan on medium-low heat, stirring constantly. Grind all spices together with the nuts in a food processor or mill. Store in an airtight container.

163

Spice Mixtures

HOGGAR CURRY SEASONING

2 tsps black peppercorns
2 tsps whole cloves
1/2 tsp ground pepper
1/2 tsp ginger
4 tsps nutmeg
1 tsp cinnamon

Grind the peppercorns and cloves together. Add the remainder of the spices. This particular curry seasoning is used by the Tuaregs (a Bedouin tribe) in the preparation of gazelle stew (which is delicious!). It can also be used to season lamb.

164

Spice Mixtures

DeSSeRTS

Here is a wonderful array of desserts to suit many tastes: the versatile cookie (crunchy almond wafers), puddings (chilled chestnut pudding), fruit preparations (stewed medlars or figs), tasty cakes featuring nuts, pears, or apples, pies (filled with quince or figs), and that classic meringue and egg dish: "Floating Island," or "Eggs on a Cloud With Caramel Sauce."

HILDEGARD'S COOKIES OF JOY

 September 17 is the traditional feast day of St. Hildegard, when it is tradition to make St. Hildegard's Cookies of Joy (circa 1157). The original recipe has been reconstructed from her treatise Physica.

3/4 cup butter
1 cup brown sugar
1 egg
1 tsp baking powder
1/4 tsp salt
1-1/2 cups flour (spelt flour is better)
1 tsp ground cinnamon
1 tsp ground nutmeg
1/2 tsp ground cloves

Preheat oven to 350 degrees F.

Cream butter with brown sugar. Beat eggs into the mixture. Sift the baking powder, salt, flour, cinnamon, nutmeg, and cloves together. Add 1/2 of the dry mixture to the creamed ingredients and mix. Add the remaining dry ingredients and mix thoroughly.

Grease and flour baking sheet.

Form walnut-sized balls of dough. Place on baking sheet and press flat.

Bake for 12-15 minutes until edges of cookies are golden brown.

Cool and serve.

Desserts

CHESTNUT PURÉE

1 lb chestnuts, peeled and cooked
1/2 cup butter
1/2 cup brown sugar
pinch of licorice powder
1 tbsp Kirsch

Drain the hot, cooked chestnuts and pass through a fine sieve. Add the butter and brown sugar, stirring until melted and the purée is smooth. Add the licorice powder and Kirsch. Pour into a mold lined with parchment paper and refrigerate for 5 to 6 hours.

Variation: You may also add 3 1/2 ozs of grated chocolate at the same time as the butter and sugar. Stir until melted. Serves 8.

Kirsch is a clear white fruit brandy made from wild European cherries. Some of the cherry stones are used in the distilling process and impart a characteristic bitter almond flavor.

CHESTNUT CRÊPES

4 tbsps spelt flour
8 tbsps chestnut flour
2 cups milk
5 eggs
2 tbsps oil
1 tbsp brandy
pinch each of licorice powder and salt

Use same method as for regular crêpes. (See page 186.) Makes 20 crêpes.

Chestnut flour can be found in some specialty stores or online In places where chestnuts are plentiful, for example, remote parts of Italy, chestnut flour is used to make various breads, cakes, and scones.

Desserts

SPICE LOAF

1/2 cup dark honey (buckwheat)
1 rounded tbsp sugar
2 cups spelt flour
1/2 cup hot water
2 tsps anise powder
1/2 tsp mixed spices (made up of equal amounts
    of cinnamon, nutmeg, cloves, and allspice)
zest of 1 orange

In a pot, melt the honey and sugar in the hot water. Add the remaining ingredients, a little at a time, mixing well. Pour into a buttered loaf pan that has a cover (or cover tightly with foil). Bake in a slow oven (325° F) for 90 minutes. Serves 6.

FRESH FIG PIE

1 lb fresh figs, peeled and cut into strips
1 baked pie shell
2 cups crème pâtissière (see recipe on page 170)
cinnamon
honey

Season the crème pâtissière with a bit of cinnamon. Pour into the baked pie shell. Top with the fresh figs. Drizzle with honey. Bake at 325° F for 5 minutes, then broil for 3 minutes.

Desserts

RAISIN RUM CAKE

1 1/4 cups brown sugar
1 cup butter
6 eggs
2 cups spelt flour
1 tsp baking powder
3/4 cup sultana raisins soaked in rum
1/2 to 1 cup candied fruit (optional)
zest of 1 lemon

Cream the butter and sugar together. Add the eggs, one at a time, beating well after each addition. Mix the flour and baking powder together and add to the egg-butter mixture. Fold in the zest and fruit. Bake in a hot oven (450° F) for 45 minutes. When baked, remove immediately from the cake pan and cool on a rack.

STEWED MEDLAR FRUIT

2 lbs fresh, ripe medlar fruit, pitted
brown sugar
5 to 6 tbsps rum

Cook the fruit in boiling water for 15 minutes; drain and purée. Return the purée to the cooking pot and reduce by one quarter. Add equal amounts of brown sugar as purée and cook for 30 minutes, stirring constantly. About 10 minutes before the end of the cooking time, add the rum. This purée can be eaten as is or used as a base for an apple pie.

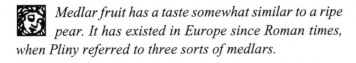 *Medlar fruit has a taste somewhat similar to a ripe pear. It has existed in Europe since Roman times, when Pliny referred to three sorts of medlars.*

169

Desserts

CRÈME PÂTISSIÈRE
(Pastry Cream Filling)

2 cups whole milk
1/3 cup brown sugar
1/2 cup spelt flour
3 egg yolks
1 tsp vanilla

Combine egg yolks with the flour, vanilla, and a little milk to moisten. Bring the remaining milk and brown sugar to a boil. While whisking constantly, carefully pour the boiling mixture over the egg-yolk mixture. Return mixture to low heat and cook, stirring constantly, until it thickens. Do not let it come to a boil. When the mixture coats the back of a wooden spoon, it is done. Refrigerate, covered with a piece of plastic wrap placed directly on the surface to prevent the formation of a skin. This cream may be used as a cake filling, for éclairs, cream puffs, and so on.

Note: If the mixture does boil, remove it from the heat and beat with a mixer until smooth.

For orange-flavored pastry cream, infuse the zest of an orange in the milk. For coffee-flavored pastry cream, add strong coffee to taste just before use, omitting the vanilla.

170

Desserts

THREE-GINGER COOKIES

3/4 cup butter
1 cup brown sugar
1/4 cup molasses
1 egg
2 cups spelt flour
1 tsp baking soda
1 tbsp ground ginger
1/2 tsp salt
1 tbsp chopped fresh ginger
1/2 cup finely chopped crystallized ginger

Cream together butter and sugar. Beat in molasses and egg. Sift together flour, baking soda, ground ginger, and salt; add to the butter mixture. Add the fresh ginger and crystallized ginger, stirring well. Refrigerate, covered, for 2 hours or overnight. Preheat oven to 350° F. Drop 1-inch balls of dough onto greased cookie sheets and bake for about 10 minutes.

Desserts

ALMOND CRUNCHIES
(Cookies)

4 eggs
3/4 cup butter, melted
2 cups spelt flour
1 cup brown sugar
2 tsps baking powder
pinch of salt
2 cups almonds, chopped and toasted

Beat the eggs well. Add the melted butter, dry ingredients, and almonds. The mixture should hold together but not be sticky. Roll out onto a floured surface to a thickness of 1/2 inch. Cut into desired shapes. Place on a baking sheet, leaving space between the cookies as they will rise. Bake in a hot oven (400–450° F) until lightly browned.

ALMOND COOKIES

1 1/4 cups finely ground almonds
3/4 cup spelt flour
2/3 cup brown sugar
1 egg

Mix all ingredients together until you have a smooth dough. Roll out onto a floured surface to a thickness of about 1 inch. Cut into desired shapes. Place on a baking sheet and bake in a moderate oven (350° F) until lightly browned.

Desserts

NO-BAKE CHOCOLATE CHESTNUT BALLS

....

1 lb chestnuts, cooked, puréed, and cooled
3 tbsps brown sugar
2 tbsps butter
1 tsp vanilla extract
4 ozs chocolate, melted
cocoa powder

Add the butter, sugar, and vanilla to the chestnut purée. Form into small balls and dip into the melted chocolate. Roll in the cocoa powder. Refrigerate.

LAVENDER-ALMOND SWEETMEATS

....

7 ozs almond paste, canned
1/4 cup lavender flowers, crushed
1/4 cup ground almonds
1/2 tsp zest of orange, grated
finely granulated sugar

Combine almond paste and lavender flowers in a small bowl. Mix well and form into 3/4-inch balls. In a separate dish, combine ground almonds and orange zest. Roll each ball in the almond mixture, and then in the granulated sugar. Refrigerate.

Desserts

STEWED FIGS IN WINE

1 lb dried figs
2 cups "Wine for the Heart" (see page 60)
1/2 tsp each cinnamon and licorice powder

Soak the dried figs in the wine overnight. Cook mixture until the figs are tender. Remove from heat and add the spices. Refrigerate. Serves 6.

CHILLED CHESTNUT PUDDING

2 lbs chestnuts, peeled
milk
3/4 cup brown sugar
9 tbsps butter
1/2 cup brandy
1 1/2 cups caramel sauce (optional)

Cook the chestnuts in milk to cover for 45 minutes. Drain and discard the milk. Purée the chestnuts. Add the sugar and butter to the purée, as well as the brandy and caramel sauce (optional). Mix well. Refrigerate overnight. Serves 6.

For the caramel sauce: Combine 1/2 pound caramels with 1 cup evaporated milk in the top of a double boiler. Stir over hot water until melted.

Desserts

CHESTNUT FLAN

1 1/2 cups chestnuts, peeled, cooked, and mashed
1 cup brown sugar
4 eggs
2 cups whole milk
dash of Kirsch brandy

Mix the mashed chestnuts with the eggs and milk. Add the brown sugar and Kirsch. Pour into a caramelized flan pan (or a pie shell). Bake in a moderate oven (325–400° F) for 30 to 40 minutes. Serves 6.

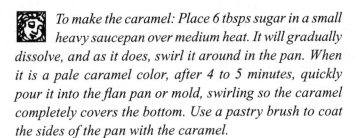 *To make the caramel: Place 6 tbsps sugar in a small heavy saucepan over medium heat. It will gradually dissolve, and as it does, swirl it around in the pan. When it is a pale caramel color, after 4 to 5 minutes, quickly pour it into the flan pan or mold, swirling so the caramel completely covers the bottom. Use a pastry brush to coat the sides of the pan with the caramel.*

HOMEMADE CREAM CHEESE

2 cups tepid milk
1 tsp rennet
1 tsp licorice

Make sure that the mixing bowl is at room temperature. Mix the tepid milk with the rennet and licorice. Place bowl in a warm place, free from drafts. After a few hours, you will see that the mixture has formed into a solid ball (curd) suspended in liquid (whey). Remove the curd and drain well. Refrigerate. You may serve this cheese as is, as a spread, for cooking, or so on, as you would regular commercial cream cheese.

175

Desserts

MAURSOIS NUT CAKE

2 1/2 cups nuts, finely ground
3/4 cup sugar
2 eggs, beaten
1/2 cup butter, softened
1/2 cup heavy cream
1 tbsp cornstarch

Mix the ground nuts with the sugar. Add 1 egg, beat until smooth, add the second egg, beat well. Add the softened butter, cream, and cornstarch; mix well. Bake in a flat cake pan for 30 minutes in a moderate oven (325–400° F).

This cake may be eaten as is: it is rich and moist.

Variation: You may also pour this batter into a baked pie shell and bake for 45 to 50 minutes.

NUT CAKE

3 eggs
2/3 cup brown sugar
1/4 cup Kirsch brandy
3/4 cup spelt flour
1 tsp baking powder
1 3/4 cups nuts, finely chopped
5 tbsps butter, melted

Beat the eggs, sugar, and Kirsch together until creamy. Add the dry ingredients and nuts, mix well. Incorporate the melted butter. Pour the batter into a buttered cake pan and bake at 350° F for 1 hour, or until done. Serves 6.

Desserts

PEAR CAKE

3 eggs
1 tbsp water
3/4 cup spelt flour
3/4 cup brown sugar
3 tbsps oil
pinch of salt
1 tsp baking powder
1 lb (3 medium) ripe pears, peeled and cut into eighths
1/3 cup butter
1 tsp vanilla
1 tsp cinnamon
pinch of licorice powder

Part 1: (For the Cake) Beat 1 egg with the water, 1/2 cup brown sugar, flour, oil, salt, and baking powder. Pour into a large buttered pie plate or cake pan. Arrange pears on top. Bake for 25 to 30 minutes in a 400° F oven.

Part 2: (For the Sauce) Melt the butter together with the remaining 1/4 cup brown sugar and 2 eggs; mix well. Add the cinnamon, vanilla, and licorice powder. Simmer until the mixture thickens while stirring constantly.

Part 3: After the cake has baked (as in Part 1), pour the sauce (made in Part 2) over it. Return to oven and bake for an additional 20 to 25 minutes at 350° F, or until done. Serves 6.

Desserts

APPLE CAKE

1 cup spelt flour
3/4 cup brown sugar
1 tsp baking powder
pinch each of licorice powder and salt
3 eggs
1 tbsp rum
4 apples, peeled and finely chopped

Mix the dry ingredients together. Add the eggs, one at a time, mixing well after each addition. Add the rum. Place the apples in the bottom of a pie plate and cover with the batter. Bake in a moderate oven (325–400° F) for 30 to 45 minutes. Serves 6.

ZUCCHINI CAKE

1 3/4 cups zucchini, unpeeled, grated
1 tbsp vanilla extract
3/4 cup nut oil
3 eggs, beaten
3 cups spelt flour
2 cups brown sugar
1 tbsp crystallized ginger
2 tsps cinnamon
1 tsp baking powder
1 1/2 cups nuts, chopped

Mix the grated zucchini with the vanilla, oil, and eggs. Combine the dry ingredients, nuts, and seasonings. Add to the zucchini mixture, a little at a time, mixing well. Pour into a large buttered cake pan and bake in at 350° F for 1 hour. Serves 10.

178

Desserts

COUNTRY-STYLE APPLE CAKE

4 apples, peeled, cored, and sliced
3/4 cup spelt flour
1 tsp baking powder
pinch of salt
1/2 cup brown sugar
juice of 1 orange
2 eggs
1 tsp oil
2/3 cup milk
quince or apple jelly

Place the sliced apples into a buttered ovenproof dish. Set aside.

Make the batter as follows: Combine the flour, baking powder, salt, sugar, orange juice, eggs, oil, and milk in that order. Mix until smooth. Pour over the apples and bake in a low-moderate oven (325–350° F) for 15 minutes. Glaze with the jelly. Serves 6.

 Quince purée is a traditional ingredient in apple pie in English cooking.

Desserts

JELLY ROLL

3 eggs, separated
1/2 cup brown sugar
1 cup spelt flour
confectioners' sugar for sprinkling

Beat the egg yolks with the sugar until creamy. Add the flour. In a separate bowl, beat the egg whites until stiff. Fold beaten egg whites into the yolk mixture. Pour the batter onto a rectangular baking sheet that has been lined with buttered parchment paper or foil. Bake for 8 to 10 minutes at 350° F. Immediately remove cake from the baking sheet, turning onto a cloth that has been lightly dusted with sugar. Remove paper or foil. Immediately spread the filling of your choice (jam, pie filling, cream) over the cake and roll (in the cloth) while still warm to prevent cracking. Refrigerate before serving. Dust with additional powdered sugar before serving. Serves 6.

 Don't spread the cake batter in the pan with a spatula. That will knock the air out of the batter.

180

Desserts

ANGELICA ICE CREAM

4 eggs, separated
3/4 cup brown sugar
zest of 1 lemon
1 cup heavy cream
2 tbsps angelica liqueur

Beat the egg yolks and sugar until creamy. Add the zest, cream, and liqueur. In a separate bowl, beat the egg whites until stiff. Fold beaten whites into yolk mixture until well combined. Pour into an ice-cream maker and freeze to harden. Serves 6.

CHESTNUT ICE CREAM

2 cups English cream (see page 182)
2 cups sweetened chestnut purée
2 tbsps angelica liqueur
1 tsp licorice powder

Mix the English cream with the chestnut purée. Add the liqueur and the licorice powder; mix well. Freeze in an ice-cream maker. Serves 6.

Desserts

ENGLISH CREAM

6 egg yolks
1 1/4 cups sugar
pinch of salt
2 cups scalded milk
dash of vanilla

Cook the egg yolks, sugar, and salt over low heat, preferably in a double boiler, stirring constantly with a spatula until the mixture forms ribbons when the spatula is lifted. Gradually add the scalded milk and vanilla, stirring constantly. Increase the heat to medium and continue stirring until bubbles almost break the surface. The cream should be thick and coat the back of the spoon. Pass mixture through a fine sieve. When cooling, stir occasionally or cover with a piece of plastic wrap placed directly on the surface of the cream to prevent the formation of a skin. Makes 2 cups.

CARAMEL SEMOLINA

2 cups milk
1 vanilla bean
1/3 cup brown sugar
4 tbsps spelt semolina
2 tbsps butter
candied fruit or currants
pinch of angelica
caramel sauce (optional: see page 174)

Bring the milk, vanilla bean, and sugar to a boil. Add the semolina all at once. Reduce heat to low and simmer for 15 minutes, stirring occasionally. Add the butter. Add the fruit of your choice and the angelica. Pour into a deep bowl, drizzle with the caramel sauce, if desired. Refrigerate before serving. Serves 4.

Desserts

"LE SAINT CURIAT"
(Chestnut Soufflé)

....

1 lb chestnuts, peeled and pitted
milk to cover the chestnuts
1 vanilla bean, slit
1/3 cup butter
1/3 cup brown sugar
4 eggs, separated
pinch of licorice powder
brandy

Cook the chestnuts in the milk with the vanilla bean for 45 minutes. Drain, remove the vanilla bean and purée. To the purée, add the butter, brown sugar, and the egg yolks, beating well.

In a separate bowl, beat the egg whites until stiff. Carefully fold whites into chestnut mixture. Pour into a buttered soufflé dish, no more than two-thirds full. You may have to tie a collar of waxed paper around the outside of the dish to support the souffle as it rises. Bake in a bain-marie (see page 211) at 375° F for 40 minutes. Serve with English Cream to which a small amount of brandy and licorice powder has been added, sweeten with honey to taste. Serves 6.

Desserts

PUMPKIN MARMALADE

4 lbs pumpkin, peeled and cut into thin strips
3 1/2 cups brown sugar
1/2 cup water
zest of 4 lemons, minced
3/4 cup rum
1 tbsp vanilla
2 1/2 tbsps licorice powder
juice of 4 lemons

Put the pumpkin, sugar, and water into a heavy pot and cook for about 20 minutes at low heat, stirring constantly, until the sugar reaches the ribbon stage. Add the lemon zest, vanilla, rum, and licorice powder. When the marmalade comes to a boil, beat until it has the consistency of applesauce. Add the lemon juice and cook for 2 to 3 minutes more, watching carefully so that it doesn't burn.

 Clean the seeds from the pumpkin, being sure to separate them from the membrane surrounding them. Soak in salt water, and roast in a low oven for a delicious snack.

Desserts

EGGS IN A CLOUD WITH CARAMEL SAUCE

6 eggs, separated
1 1/4 cups brown sugar
1 tsp licorice powder
3 cups whole milk
caramel sauce (see page 174)

Part 1: (For the Custard) Beat the 6 egg yolks with 3/4 cup sugar and licorice powder. Add the milk, a little at a time, beating constantly. Cook over low heat, stirring constantly, just until it begins to bubble. Immediately remove from heat and continue to stir for 30 strokes. Pour into a deep flat serving bowl. Chill.

Part 2: (For the Meringue) Beat the egg whites until very stiff, add the remainder of the sugar, beat again until the sugar is dissolved. Fill a flat pan with boiling water. When the water begins to bubble, add the meringue to it by spoonfuls. Poach the meringues, turning until they are cooked evenly on all sides. Remove from water, drain well. Chill.

Part 3: (For the Assembly) When both the custard and meringues are chilled, carefully place the meringues on top of the custard. Drizzle your favorite caramel sauce over the finished dish. Serves 6.

 To make powdered licorice: grind dried licorice stems into powder in a spice grinder.

Desserts

BASIC CRÊPE BATTER

1 cup spelt flour
3 eggs
1 1/4 cups scalded milk
3 tbsps cream
1/2 tsp licorice powder
orgeat syrup or Kirsch or rum to taste

Beat the flour with one egg and a little milk to make a smooth batter. Continue beating and add the other 2 eggs, the remainder of the milk, cream, licorice powder, and the syrup. Beat until well mixed. Cover and refrigerate overnight.

Lightly oil a crêpe pan or flat frying pan. Pour in a small amount of batter, moving the pan around to coat the entire surface uniformly. After a few seconds, lift the edge to see if the underside is brown. If so, turn the crêpe to brown the second side. Remove from pan. Continue with the remainder of the batter. If the first crêpe seems dry, add a little milk to the batter; if it's too liquid, add a little flour to the batter. This will make 15 to 20 crêpes. If you are using the crêpes for main dishes, omit the syrup (or the spirits) and replace with a pinch of cumin.

 Orgeat syrup is a sweet nonalcoholic syrup made from almonds and sugar with rose water or orange-flower water, used to flavor drinks or food.

Desserts

ALMOND MERINGUES

1 1/4 cups almonds, very finely ground
2/3 cup brown sugar
2 egg whites
candied angelica, finely chopped

Combine the almonds and sugar. In a separate bowl, beat the egg whites until stiff. Add to the almonds and sugar. Spoon into a pastry bag. Pipe out into small disks onto a buttered baking sheet. Decorate each with a small piece of angelica. Bake in a slow oven (275° F) until set. When done, paint each meringue with sweetened milk.

PLUM PUDDING

9 tbsps butter, softened
3/4 cup granulated sugar
pinch of salt
3 eggs
1 1/4 cups spelt flour
1/2 cup raisins, soaked in rum
1/2 cup candied fruit
1 tsp baking powder
zest of 1 lemon

Cream the butter and sugar until well blended, add the salt. Add eggs, one at a time, beating after each addition. Continue beating; add the flour, aerating the batter as much as possible. Add the rum-soaked raisins, candied fruit, baking powder, and lemon zest. Pour into a buttered baking mold and bake in at 375° F for 45 minutes to an hour. Serve with your favorite sauce. Serves 6.

Desserts

PEARS STEWED IN WINE

2 lbs pears (6 medium), peeled and quartered
4 cups "Wine for the Heart" (see page 60)
2 tbsps brown sugar
1/2 tsp each cinnamon and licorice powder

Poach the pears in the wine, sugar, and spices for 30 minutes. Add additional brown sugar to taste. Chill before serving. Serves 6.

INDIAN-STYLE APPLES

1 tbsp vegetable oil
5 whole cloves
1 tsp each of freshly grated ginger, cinnamon,
　　fenugreek, anthemis (optional)
1 small hot pepper, cut in half, seeded and sliced
2 lbs (6 medium) apples, peeled and chopped
　　into small pieces
1 tsp each of galingale, licorice powder
3/4 cup water
3/4 cup brown sugar

Heat the oil in a frying pan and sauté the cloves, ginger, cinnamon, fenugreek, anthemis, and the pepper. Add the apples, galingale, and licorice powder; continue to cook for a few minutes. Add the water and boil for 5 minutes. Reduce heat and simmer for 12 minutes, watching that the apples do not stick. Add the sugar and simmer until the mixture gels. You may serve this cold as a dessert or warm as an accompaniment for poultry. Serves 6.

Desserts

BAKED APPLES

apples, peeled and cored
chopped nuts
butter
raisins soaked in rum
quince or other tart fruit jelly
brown sugar

Use 1 apple per person. Plug the bottoms of the apples with a mixture of butter and chopped nuts. Fill the centers with the soaked raisins. Close the tops with a mixture of quince jelly and brown sugar. Place the stuffed apples in a baking dish, adding a little water. Prick the apples so they don't burst while baking. Bake in a moderate oven (350° F) for 35 minutes or until done.

QUINCE PIE

5 quinces, peeled and sliced
juice of 1 lemon
1 baked pie shell
2 eggs
2 cups milk
1/3 cup brown sugar
1/2 tsp licorice powder
cinnamon

Prepare the quinces and sprinkle with the lemon juice. Place the quince slices in bottom of baked pie shell. In a separate bowl, beat the eggs with the milk, brown sugar, and licorice powder and pour over the quince slices. Sprinkle with cinnamon. Bake at 375° F for 40 to 50 minutes. This pie may be served hot or cold. You may glaze the pie with quince jelly, if desired. Serves 6.

189

Desserts

SYRuPS aND LiQueURS

Hildegard's kitchen featured many homemade syrups and liqueurs. A syrup is a sweetened liquid often made with fruits or herbs. It is often used as a flavoring for desserts or as an ingredient for nonalcoholic drinks diluted with soda, water, or even lemonade. A liqueur (an alcoholic spirit distilled with some form of fruit or herb or other flavoring substance) is sweet. Fruit syrups preserve the concentrated essence of their ingredients and make ideal pantry staples for a variety of uses.

"The person who does good works sees God,
but the one who has a mere thought about good works
is like a mirror in which an image is reflected,
but the image is not really there. So rise up and
begin good works and bring them to perfection,
and God will receive you."

St. Hildegard of Bingen

SAINT CLEMENT'S CORDIAL

juice of 8 oranges, about 3 cups
juice of 6 lemons
zest of 2 oranges and 2 lemons
4 1/2 cups granulated sugar

Combine the fruit juices and zest in a saucepan along with the sugar. Stir over low heat until the sugar has dissolved. Turn up the heat and bring almost to the boiling point. Remove from the heat and let cool.

Strain the liquid through a double layer of cheesecloth and pour into clean bottles. Seal and refrigerate.

LIQUEUR OF LOVE

2 cups brandy
2 3/4 cups brown sugar
1 vanilla bean, slit
1 lemon, cut into quarters
2 cups heavy cream or whole milk

Combine all ingredients together in a large jar. Shake thoroughly until well mixed. Let sit for 24 days, stirring occasionally. Filter through filter paper and put into a clean bottle.

 This recipe is a version of the Gaelic liqueur bain-necor which means "milk of the heart."

Syrups & Liqueurs

SPICED WINE

1 tsp freshly grated ginger
4 cinnamon sticks, broken in thirds
4 cardamom seeds, coarsely ground
1/2 cup sugar
1/8 tsp pepper
4 cups red wine
lemon slices

Place spices and sugar in a large pot and pour in the wine. Bring to a boil and simmer, tightly covered for 5 to 7 minutes. Remove all the whole spices and serve warm in goblets or small glass bowls. Garnish each with a slice of fresh lemon. Refrigerate any wine that is left over.

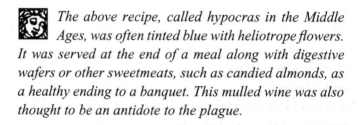 *The above recipe, called hypocras in the Middle Ages, was often tinted blue with heliotrope flowers. It was served at the end of a meal along with digestive wafers or other sweetmeats, such as candied almonds, as a healthy ending to a banquet. This mulled wine was also thought to be an antidote to the plague.*

Syrups & Liqueurs

NUT WINE

25 young nuts, cut into quarters (about 3 to 4 ozs)
5 qts (20 cups) red wine
1 qt (4 cups) brandy
2 lbs (5 cups) brown sugar

Pick the nuts around the middle of June, making sure that they have a green, milky flavor. Soak the nuts in the wine and brandy for 1 month, stirring occasionally. At the end of the month, remove 1 qt (4 cups) of the juice and dissolve the sugar in it. When the sugar is fully dissolved, pour back into the mixture. Let sit for 3 months. Filter and bottle.

QUINCE LIQUEUR

6 lbs quince fruit, unpeeled and grated
1 cup lightly packed brown sugar
2 tbsps milk
vodka or food-grade alcohol

Pour the milk over the grated quince, mix well, and let ferment for 48 hours. Strain and measure the juice produced. For each 4 cups of liquid, add 1 cup brown sugar which has been dissolved in a small amount of water. Pour into bottles, adding an equal amount of alcohol or vodka. Mix well.

Dreaming of quinces is reputed to foretell good luck, and in case you are in the company of anyone who has accidentally swallowed a deadly poison, the juice of a raw quince is an antidote, or so says Nicholas Culpeper in The English Physitian *(1652).*

Syrups & Liqueurs

NUT LIQUEUR

30 young nuts, preferably green
1 qt (4 cups) brandy
1 cup lightly packed brown sugar
2 whole cloves
cinnamon, nutmeg to taste

Around the middle of June, pick the young nuts. Ensure that they are tender and moist, with a green, milky flavor. Crush them well with a mortar and pestle, or grind them coarsely in a food processor. Put this into a crockery bowl or container with the brandy, cloves, cinnamon, and nutmeg. Let sit for 30 days. Strain the liquid through a double thickness of cheesecloth. Measure the liquid and add 1 cup dissolved brown sugar per qt of liquid. Mix well. Let sit for an additional 15 days. Filter and pour into bottles.

 *Hazelnuts are a good choice for this recipe. In the Middle Ages, divining rods made of hazelwood were used to find unseen streams of water or hidden treasure.*

Syrups & Liqueurs

PEACH LEAF LIQUEUR

120 peach leaves (about 1 qt lightly packed), unwilted,
with no signs of disease, and from unsprayed trees
1 cup brandy
1 qt (4 cups) red wine
2 1/2 cups lightly packed brown sugar

Crush the peach leaves and put them into a crock along with the wine, brandy, and sugar for 8 days. Filter and bottle. Let sit for 2 to 3 months before using.

 This recipe may be varied by adding 10 peach pits in with the leaves. This imparts a nutty, slightly bitter taste to the liqueur. Another variant can be made by adding 2 to 3 handfuls of scented rose petals.

SAGE LIQUEUR

1 cup sage leaves and flowers, or more to taste
1 qt (4 cups) brandy
2 cups lightly packed brown sugar
2 cups water

Soak the sage leaves and flowers in the brandy in a crock for 8 days, stirring well with a wooden spoon and macerating the sage against the sides of the container. Strain through cheesecloth. Prepare a syrup consisting of water and brown sugar. Boil syrup for 15 minutes. Add to the strained sage liquid. Mix well. Bottle and allow to age before using.

 A medieval folk story says that when the Blessed Virgin began her flight to Egypt, she hid from Herod's soldiers among sage plants and was not seen by her pursuers. She blessed the plant, and ever since then its leaves have been fragrant.

Syrups & Liqueurs

FLAXSEED SYRUP

4 1/2 ozs flaxseeds
4 cups water
2 cups honey
juice of 3 lemons

Prepare a decoction, using the flaxseeds and water. Boil for 1 minute. Add the lemon juice and honey. This syrup is good when you have a cold. Drink a glass of it a few times a day until the cold passes.

> *A decoction is an extraction process used for seeds, roots, and berries that require a longer time or higher heat to release their flavors or other properties. Usually, the selected material is boiled in a liquid, some of which is allowed to evaporate. Decoctions should be used fairly soon after they are prepared.*

Syrups & Liqueurs

JaMS aND JeLLieS

The preserving of fruits with sugar was a part of the domestic tradition in a medieval kitch-en. Here are some familiar and some not-so-familiar recipes for jams and jellies that grow out of that waste-not-want-not school of cooking. Forma-tion of a skin is the last step in jam and jelly making. To test for a skin, put a small amount of the cooked mixture onto a saucer. If you lift up the spoon and the mixture drips from it at long intervals and in large drops, it has reached the "skin" stage and is ready. Alternately, drizzle some of the jelly liquid on a cold plate and place it in the refrigerator for 1 to 2 minutes. If it has thickened so that it doesn't run all over the plate, it is ready.

Special Instructions to Note About the Procedures Used in Jam and Jelly Making

1. To check if the jelly or jam is done, drop some onto a plate. If it gels right away, it is done (see page 199).

2. Put the jam or jelly into the hot, sterilized jars when the mixture is hot, and seal the jars.

3. In most cases, you may use the food processor or blender to make jelly. This helps eliminate the fruit seeds. It is a quicker method, but it will make a jelly that is thicker than if you use a food mill to grind the fruit.

4. Some people may choose to reduce the sugar used in the recipes to 1 to 1 1/4 pounds per 2 pounds of fruit. If you decide to do so, let the mixture cook at low heat for an additional hour and pour into hot sterilized jars. Cover the jam/jelly when it is still hot.

CHESTNUT JAM

peeled chestnuts
1 vanilla bean, slit
salted water
brown sugar
1 to 2 cups water

Cover the peeled chestnuts with salted water and cook for 30 minutes with the vanilla bean. Remove the bean, drain, and purée the cooked chestnuts until smooth. Measure the amount of purée and add an equal amount of brown sugar and 1 to 2 cups water (depending on your personal taste and thickness desired). Boil, stirring constantly, until the mixture is translucent. Pour into hot sterilized jars.

 Already puréed chestnuts are available in cans.

MILK JAM

1 qt (4 cups) whole milk
5 1/2 cups brown sugar
1 vanilla bean, slit
3 whole cloves
cinnamon to taste
2 tbsps rum

Melt the sugar in the milk; add the vanilla bean and cloves. Bring to a boil, reduce heat and simmer at low heat for 50 minutes, stirring occasionally. Remove the vanilla bean and cloves, add the cinnamon and rum and continue simmering for 10 minutes. Mix well. Pour into hot sterilized jars.

ROSE HIP JAM

rose hips, approximately 4 cups
water
sugar

Choose rose hips that are ripe and a good red color. Cut the green parts off each end and split in half lengthwise. Scrape and clean under running water to remove the seeds and fluff, which may give a bad taste to the jam. Soak the rose hips in a little water for 4 to 5 days until tender. They may be a little fermented. Drain and purée. Measure the purée and add an equal amount of sugar. Boil approximately 45 to 60 minutes or until the jam has a good color and appears to be like a liquid purée. Pour into hot sterilized jars.

Hips can be gathered from any rosebush, wild or cultivated. Collect them after the first frost, which softens their texture and their sour taste. They have a high pectin content, and make attractive sunset-colored jellies and syrups. Rose hips are also available dried at many herb and health-food stores.

BLACKBERRY JELLY

ripe blackberries
water
brown sugar
juice of 1 lemon

Measure the amount of fruit, adding 1/2 cup water per quart (4 cups) of fruit. Boil the mixture in a heavy pot for a few minutes, mashing the fruit. Strain through a cheesecloth. Measure the juice, return to the pot and add brown sugar (in a proportion of 90 percent of the amount of juice). Add the lemon juice and boil until a skin forms, about 20 to 30 minutes. Pour into hot sterilized jars.

Jams & Jellies

FIG JAM

fresh figs
boiling water
brown sugar

Choose figs that are not too ripe and are of similar size. Prick them with a fork so they don't burst. Add figs to boiling water to cover and let soak for 10 minutes. Drain. Measure and add sugar and water in the following proportions: 2 cups brown sugar and 1 cup water for each lb of figs. Cook mixture until skin forms. (See page 199.) Rub mixture through a coarse sieve, and return it to the pan to reheat through before pouring into hot sterilized jars.

Note: Dried figs may be substituted in this recipe. In this case, steam the dried figs until soft, and proceed to measure and cook according to the instructions.

The fig tree is considered sacred to Hindus and Buddhists for whom it represents knowledge and enlightenment. In India, the bark of the fig tree is used to treat skin diseases and inflamed feet.

GOOSEBERRY JELLY

gooseberries
water
brown sugar

Remove the gooseberries from their stems with a fork. Rinse well. Measure the amount of fruit and, in a heavy pot, add 1/2 cup water per quart of fruit. Cook for a few minutes, stir often and mash the fruit with a fork. Strain the fruit through a cheesecloth, squeezing to remove all the juice. Measure the juice, return it to the pot, adding an equal amount of sugar (which has already been dissolved in a small amount of hot water). Cook until a skin forms, removing any foam produced. Pour into hot sterilized jars.

203

Jams & Jellies

WALNUT JAM

50 or so young walnuts
water
brown sugar

Pick the walnuts around the middle of June when they are hard,
green, and small. Don't use any that cannot be pierced by a pin.
(Green nuts contain a liquid that shoots out when the nut is pricked.)
Soak in water for 15 to 20 days, changing the water every morning.
Boil the nuts in fresh water until they are tender and have detached
from their shells. Drain, rinse in cold water, drain again. Measure
the amount of fruit and add an equal amount of brown sugar with
a small amount of water. Bring to a boil, reduce heat, and simmer
for 7 to 8 hours at low heat. Pour into hot sterilized jars.

ONION JAM

2 lbs onions, peeled and minced
1/2 cup butter
salt, pepper to taste
2/3 cup brown sugar
1/2 cup white wine
1/2 cup vinegar
1/2 cup blackberry or black currant liqueur

Sweat the onions in the butter, season with salt and pepper. Simmer at low heat for 20 minutes until transparent. Add the brown
sugar and simmer for 8 to 10 minutes. Add the wine, vinegar, and
liqueur. Cook at medium heat for 1 hour. Cook the onions slowly,
stirring often to make sure that they don't burn, which may cause
them to give off an acrid flavor. Let cool and refrigerate. This jam
may be served on crackers or to accompany a meat dish, such as
a hearty stew.

Jams & Jellies

QUINCE JELLY

quince fruit, peeled and cut into eighths
juice of 1 orange and 1 lemon
water
brown sugar

Measure the amount of fruit. Add 1 quart (4 cups) of water for each 1 pound of fruit. Bring the quince fruit, water, and citrus juice to a boil and simmer until the fruit breaks apart. Strain the mixture, keeping the juice. Put the fruit aside. (See note below.) Measure the juice, return to the pot, and add an equal amount of brown sugar. Continue to cook, removing the foam produced, until a skin forms. Strain again, if necessary, and bottle in hot sterilized jars.

Note: The cooked fruit pulp may be used as follows: add to an equal amount of applesauce, 1/2 tsp licorice powder, a pinch of cinnamon, 1/2 cup brown sugar. Let sit for 4 to 5 hours. Pour into a buttered and sugared ovenproof dish and bake in a slow oven (250° F) for 3 to 4 hours. Chill and serve with English Cream (see page 182).

Raw quince fruit is hard and stays that way until it has been cooked, when the flesh turns pink. Quince is one of the oldest cultivated plants; and a quince syrup was often drunk as a treatment for sore throats.

DANDELION JELLY

1 1/2 qts dandelion flowers, without stems
4 cups brown sugar
1 1/2 qts (6 cups) water
2 oranges, unpeeled and sliced
1 lemon, unpeeled and sliced
few drops of vanilla extract

Make sure that the green part of the dandelion is peeled from the base of the flower, since the green part is quite bitter. Dry the flowers. Soak overnight in the water, adding the orange and lemon slices. Bring mixture to a boil, reduce heat, and simmer for 1 hour, ensuring that the dandelion flowers are well immersed in the liquid. Sieve through a cheesecloth and squeeze to make sure that all the liquid is extracted. Return juice to the pot, add the brown sugar and vanilla. Simmer for 45 minutes or until a skin forms, stirring occasionally. Strain through cheesecloth, if necessary, and pour into hot sterilized jars.

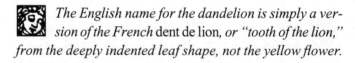 *The English name for the dandelion is simply a version of the French* dent de lion, *or "tooth of the lion," from the deeply indented leaf shape, not the yellow flower.*

ELDERBERRY JELLY

elderberries
brown sugar
juice of 2 lemons

Purée the fruit in a food mill twice, finishing with the finest mesh. Strain the processed fruit through a cheesecloth, squeezing well. Make sure that there are no seeds. (See note below). Measure and pour the juice into a heavy pot, adding an equal amount of brown sugar and the lemon juice. Cook until a skin forms. Pour into hot sterilized jars.

Note: Do not purée elderberries in a food processor or blender— the seeds are poisonous.

206

Jams & Jellies

TABLE GRACES FROM SAINT BENEDICT AND OTHERS

We praise you, God, Our Father,
For you give us not only the earth's bounty,
but also your living Word.
Grant us the grace to eat our meal in thanksgiving,
and make us worthy to take part
in the feast of your wisdom.
Through Our Lord, Jesus Christ. Amen.

God, Our Father,
We continually want to thank you,
because you shower us with your riches.
Whether we eat or drink,
give us the grace to do everything to glorify you
and to always give thanks to you.
Through Our Lord, Jesus Christ. Amen.

Table Graces

Blessed are you, Lord, Our God,
As you give food to all living creatures;
open our hearts and make them generous,
so that we may glorify you,
and joyfully share what you have given us.
Through Our Lord, Jesus Christ. Amen.

We give thanks to you, Our Father,
For this meal which brings us closer together.
Give us the grace to have our meal
with joy and a simplicity of heart;
make us faithful in our daily praise of you,
in loving friendship and brotherly charity.
Through Our Lord, Jesus Christ. Amen.

Blessed are you, Lord, Our God,
Through your Son Jesus who took on our weakness
to give us his strength.
Grant us the grace to eat this meal in joy
and thanksgiving.
Through Our Lord, Jesus Christ. Amen.

Lord, Our Father,
You make the seed germinate,
and the harvest come to fruition;
blessed are you, for the food you give us;
grant us the grace to, one day, sit with all the saints
at the celestial table in your kingdom.
Forevermore. Amen.

Table Graces

Heavenly Father,
Thank you for this meal in the company
of our brothers and sisters in Christ.
And since we do not live by bread alone,
make us hunger for your Word,
now and forever.
Through Our Lord, Jesus Christ. Amen.

Lord, Our God,
In your great charity,
you give us Fatherly help;
bless us and this food we are about to eat.
In your kindness, make it so that all peoples
abundantly benefit from your providential generosity.
Through Our Lord, Jesus Christ. Amen.

Lord, we thank you.
Everything that is good comes from you;
bless the food in this community meal
and give us the grace to be united
with you and those sharing this meal, forever. Amen

Table Graces

Glossary and Measurements

Tips

○ If you use chestnuts in the shell, refrigerate them for 24 hours then plunge them into boiling water. This will facilitate removal of the double layer of shell and skin at the same time.

○ In terms of fats and oils used in cooking, use what you like—vegetable oil, butter, or margarine—but use good quality products.

○ Herbs mentioned in the recipes may be used fresh or in their dried form. Adjust the quantities accordingly.

Cooking Terms Used

Bain-Marie: A method of cooking certain delicate foods gently by lowering a casserole or other cooking vessel containing the food to be cooked into a flat pan with sides higher than the casserole, half filled with hot water.

Blanching: An operation consisting of plunging meat or vegetables into boiling water to tenderize, clean, or eliminate the acidity. Times vary depending upon the food being blanched.

Bouquet Garni: Aromatic herbs or plants tied together in a little bundle, used to season soups, stews, or sauces during cooking and removed at the end of the cooking time. It is usually comprised of parsley, thyme, and a bay leaf. The proportions and amounts are adjusted according to the nature of the dish. It may

also include basil, chervil, chives, celery, tarragon, rosemary, savory, burnet, and so on.

Browning: Sauté various cooking ingredients (meat or vegetables) in hot oil or butter to firm or color the surface.

Caramelize: Usually used to coat a mold into which a cream or other mixture is to be poured for cooking. To prepare the caramel, put sugar with a few drops of water into a heavy pan and heat until the sugar begins to melt and begins to turn brown in color. Carefully pour (this is extremely hot) into the cooking dish (it may also be brushed onto the dish). When the caramel has hardened, pour in the custard and chill overnight. The caramel will melt and become syrupy, facilitating removal of the custard from the mold.

Court-Bouillon: A liquid generally consisting of salted water into which wine, vinegar or milk, carrots, onions, and a bouquet garni have been added. Used to cook fish or certain meats. Generally speaking, use 2 quarts or 8 cups of court-bouillon for each 1 pound of meat or fish.

Decoction: The process of boiling certain herbs and/or their parts in water in order to make an extract. If the water does not come to a boil, it is called an infusion.

Dilute: Adding a liquid to the cooking of a dish or sauce to thin it.

Etouffée: The method of cooking a mixture in a heavy covered casserole using little or no water. One may pour cold water over the outside of the cooking vessel to create condensation on the interior which will fall by small drops into the dish. This gives a particular flavor to the juices produced. Also called *à l'étuvée*.

Fines Herbes: All plants used for seasoning, such as parsley, chives, tarragon, and so on.

Gilding: Brushing a pastry with a beaten egg yolk so it browns.

Glaze: The application of a sauce, jelly, gravy, or coulis onto a dish: meat, chicken, fish, or cake.

Preliminary Notes

Marinade: A mixture used for steeping meat or fish. A typical marinade is made up of 2 cups of a full-bodied red wine, 2 sliced onions, 5 whole cloves, 1 cup cognac, 1 cup oil, 1/2 teaspoon vinegar, tarragon, parsley, bay leaf.

Marinate: The operation of placing raw meat or fish into an aromatic liquid (marinade) in order to give it a special flavor or to tenderize it.

Mixture: A combination of various ingredients generally mixed together with a sauce or cream. Mixed preparations that go into the making of certain dishes.

Pie Shell (crust): A dough which is rolled out and used as a base for a pie. May be a single (bottom) crust or double (top and bottom) crust.

Reduce: To cook by boiling at high heat to decrease the volume of sauce or cooking juices; or as a means to thicken it.

Roux: A mixture made of flour and fat used as a thickening agent for sauces. There are three kinds of roux: brown, blond, and white, depending on how much the fat and flour are browned.

Simmer: To cook slowly and gently over low heat.

Singe: The process of rotating poultry and winged game over a flame to burn off the feathers and hair.

Steep: The process of soaking food in a cold aromatic liquid. One may steep plants or fruit until their soluble parts are dissolved, for example, pickles, brandied fruit, and so on.

Thicken: The action of giving certain sauces, cooking juices, or coulis the desired density by the addition of butter, cream, egg yolk, flour, starch, and so on, as the recipe requires.

Zest: The rind of a citrus fruit, excluding the inner white skin, which is bitter.

Preliminary Notes

CONVERSIONS AND EQUIVALENTS

TEMPERATURES

Temp in F°	Temp in C°	Gas Mark	Usage
250–275	125–135	1	*meringues*
275–300	145–155	2–3	*puddings, dry cookies*
325–350	155–175	3–4	*stews, pâté, terrines*
350–375	175–195	4–5	*cakes*
375–400	195–215	5–6	*pies, soufflé, fish, vegetables*
400–450	215–235	6–7	*veal roast, flaky pastry*
450–500	235–255	7–8	*large poultry, roast beef*
500 +	255–275	8–9	*game poultry, mutton*
broil	275–295	9–10	*au gratin dishes*

Baking Temperatures	Fahrenheit°	Celsius°
Cool	225	110
	250	130
Very slow	275	140
	300	150
Slow	325	170
Moderate	350	180
	375	190
Moderately hot	400	200
Fairly hot	425	220
Hot	450	230
Very hot	475	240
Extremely hot	500	250

Preliminary Notes

SOLIDS

Ounces	Pounds	Grams
1		28
2		56
3 1/2		100
4	1/4	112
5		140
6		168
8	1/2	225
9		250
12	3/4	340
16	1	450
18		500
20	1 1/4	560
24	1 1/2	675
27		750
28	1 3/4	780
32	2	900
36	2 1/4	1000

Preliminary Notes

CONVERSIONS AND EQUIVALENTS

LIQUIDS

Fluid Ounces	U.S.	Imperial	Milliliters
	1 teaspoon	1 teaspoon	5
1/4	2 teaspoons	1 dessertspoon	10
1/2	1 tablespoon	1 tablespoon	14
1	2 tablespoons	2 tablespoons	28
2	1/4 cup	4 tablespoons	56
4	1/2 cup		110
5		1/4 pint or 1 gill	140
6	3/4 cup		170
8	1 cup		225
9			250
10	1 1/4 cups	1/2 pint	280
12	1 1/2 cups		340
15		3/4 pint	420
16	2 cups		450
18	2 1/4 cups		500
20	2 1/2 cups	1 pint	560
24	3 cups		675
25		1 1/4 pints	700
27	3 1/2 cups		750
30	3 3/4 cups	1 1/2 pints	840
32	4 cups or 1 quart		900

Preliminary Notes

SOURCES
FOR INGREDIENTS
(UPDATED 10/28/13)

The Lhasa Karnak Herb Company
2482 Telegraph Avenue
Berkeley, CA 94704

1938 Shattuck Avenue
Berkeley, CA 94704

510-548-0380
www.herb-inc.com

More than 500 different types of herbs available

Penzeys Spices
800-741-7787
penzeys.com

Retail stores throughout the U.S.

Purity Foods, Inc.
417 S. Meridian Road
Hudson, MI 49247
800-997-7358
517-448-2050
natureslegacyforlife.com/

Provider of spelt flour and grains.

San Francisco Herb Co.
250 14th Street
San Francisco, CA 94103
800-227-4530
415-861-3018
www.sfherb.com

Catalog of herbs, spices, and teas.

Sources

INDEX

Also From Liguori Publications

From a Monastery Kitchen
The Classic Natural Foods Cookbook
Brother Victor-Antoine D'Avila-Latourrette

ISBN: 978-0-7648-0850-0

Monastic cookery, as it has been practiced through the centuries, is cherished for its emphasis on simplicity, wholesome frugality, basic good taste, and the seasonal rhythms of ingredients used. Healthy eaters, practical cooks, cookbook collectors, and recipe readers will treasure this edition of this classic cookbook containing more than 125 recipes, arranged seasonally.

Twelve Months of Monastery Soups
International Favorites
Brother Victor-Antoine D'Avila-Latourrette

ISBN: 978-0-8924-3931-7

Soups have always held a very prominent place in the daily fare of monasteries. This collection of healthy recipes follows the orderly cycle of the 12 months of the year, features seasonally fresh produce, and includes basic recipes for stocks and sauces. Makes a great gift or addition to your cookbook collection.

Sacred Feasts
From a Monastery Kitchen
Brother Victor-Antoine D'Avila-Latourrette

ISBN: 978-0-7648-1862-2

This book of seasonal cooking provides a backdrop of celebrating sacred feasts of the year from a monastery kitchen to your kitchen—using recipes from Brother Victor-Antoine d'Avila-Latourrette. Brother Victor-Antoine is the best-selling author of several cookbooks from his monastery kitchen. *Sacred Feasts* focuses on using seasonal fresh fruits and vegetables to create inexpensive, delicious, healthy, and beautiful vegetarian dishes to delight your family and friends. Recipes include simple and savory desserts, main dishes, and—of course—entire meals to help celebrate feast days, family get-togethers, and to make even the most ordinary day special. This is the perfect recipe book for everyone who loves to cook and to use affordable, fresh, wholesome in-season fruits and vegetables that will please everyone!

To order visit your local bookstore or call 800-325-9521 or visit us at www.liguori.org